Theodore Roosevelt

Theodore Roosevelt, in a very presidential pose, 1903. *Library of Congress*

Theodore Roosevelt

LARGER THAN LIFE

Matt Donnelly

Linnet Books
North Haven, Connecticut

First published 2003 as a Linnet Book,
an imprint of The Shoe String Press, Inc.
2 Linsley St., North Haven, Connecticut 06473.
www.shoestringpress.com

Library of Congress Cataloging-in-Publication Data

Donnelly, Matt, 1972–
    Theodore Roosevelt : larger than life / Matt Donnelly.
        p. cm.
    Includes bibliographical references and index.
    ISBN 0–208–02510–3 (alk. paper)
        1. Roosevelt, Theodore, 1858–1919—Juvenile literature. 2. Presidents—
United States—Biography—Juvenile literature. I. Title.

    E757 .D66 2002
    973.91'1'092—dc21
    [B]   2002073061

The paper in this publication meets the
minimum requirements of American National
Standard for Information Sciences—Permanence
of Paper for Printed Library Materials,
ANSI/NISO Z39.48—1992 (R1997). ∞

Designed by Dutton & Sherman
Printed in Hong Kong by C & C Offset Printing Co., Ltd.

For Amy and Kylie,
my favorite girls

"Colonel Roosevelt . . . does everything that a man can do, and he does it well. Some biographer of the future will have a stiff job—Mr. Roosevelt does so much."[1]

CONTENTS

ILLUSTRATIONS

ACKNOWLEDGMENTS

EDITORS AND PUBLISHERS have one of the toughest jobs in the world—making writers look good. In particular I wish to thank Diantha Thorpe, the publisher of The Shoe String Press, who believed in this project from the start and slaved over the manuscript for many hours. Her patience and dedication have helped make this book what it is. Of course, all errors and oversights are of my own making.

Thank you, as well, to Wallace Dailey of the Theodore Roosevelt Association and Anna Kiefer of the Bath (Maine) Historical Society for supplying important photographs.

Last, but certainly not least, I would also like to thank my wife, Amy, and my daughter, Kylie, for allowing me the time away from family responsibilities to make this dream of mine a reality. Without you both, this book never would have seen the light of day.

A ROOSEVELT CHRONOLOGY

1858	Born in New York City
1865	Watches Abraham Lincoln's funeral procession from his grandfather's window
1876	Enrolls at Harvard College
1878	Theodore Sr., father, dies of stomach cancer
1880	June 30: Graduates from Harvard College October: Enrolls at Columbia Law School October 27: Marries Alice Lee
1881	Elected to New York State Assembly
1882	Publishes *The Naval War of 1812*
1883–1884	Establishes two cattle ranches in the Badlands
1884	February 12: Daughter, Alice, is born February 14: Wife Alice Lee and Martha Bulloch Roosevelt, mother, die
1884–1886	Operates ranches in Badlands
1886	Marries Edith Carow
1887	First son, Theodore, is born
1889	Second son, Kermit, is born
1889–1895	Serves as U.S. Civil Service Commissioner
1891	Second daughter, Ethel, is born
1894	Third son, Archibald, is born

1895–1897	Serves as Police Commissioner of New York City
1897–1898	Serves as Assistant Secretary of the Navy
1897	Fourth son, Quentin, is born
1898	Fights in Cuba with "Rough Riders" during Spanish-American War
1898–1900	Serves as Governor of New York
1900	Elected Vice President of the United States
1901	Becomes President after McKinley's death
1902	Coal strike
	June 17: Signs National Reclamation Act
1904	February: Senate ratifies Panama Canal treaty
	November: Reelected President by largest margin in American history
1905	Brokers peace treaty ending Russo-Japanese War
1906	Wins Nobel Peace Prize
	June 8: Signs National Monuments Act
1909	Leaves the White House, succeeded by Taft
1910	Goes on nationwide speaking tour
1912	Runs for President as the Progressive ("Bull Moose") Party candidate
1913	Publishes *Autobiography*
1914	Panama Canal opens
1915–1917	Rallies American support for World War I and criticizes President Wilson
1917	United States enters World War I
1918	Delivers final speech
1919	Dies of heart failure at home

INTRODUCTION

THEODORE ROOSEVELT was a man who seemed to have endless reserves of passion and energy. Only forty-three years old when he entered the White House, he was at that time the youngest president in the history of the United States, only eight years older than the minimum age set forth in the Constitution.

Roosevelt's high-octane personality was well known, both in the United States and around the world. His friend and early biographer, William Roscoe Thayer, told the story of one time when the new French ambassador to the United States, M. Jusserand, was able to experience President Roosevelt's exuberance firsthand during a hike to a wild stream near Washington called Rock Creek. "To be invited by the President to go on one of those hikes," Thayer recalled, "was regarded as a mark of special favor. He indulged in them to test a man's bodily vigor and endurance." Jusserand sent a report of his hiking trip to the French Foreign Office, which Thayer summarized:

> Yesterday President Roosevelt invited me to take a promenade with him this afternoon at three. I arrived at the White House punctually, in afternoon dress and silk hat . . . To my surprise, the President soon joined me in a tramping suit, with knickerbockers and thick boots, and soft felt hat, much worn. . . . we started off at what seemed to me a breakneck pace, which soon brought us out of the city. On reaching the country, the President went pell-mell over the fields, following neither road nor path, always on, on, straight ahead!

I was much winded, but I would not give in, nor ask him to slow up, because I had the honor of *La belle France* in my heart. At last we came to the bank of a stream, rather wide and too deep to be forded. I sighed relief, because I thought that now we had reached our goal and would rest a moment and catch our breath, before turning homeward. But judge of my horror when I saw the President unbutton his clothes and heard him say, "We had better strip, so as not to wet our things in the Creek." Then I, too, for the honor of France, removed my apparel, everything except my lavender kid gloves. The President cast an inquiring look at these as if they, too, must come off, but I quickly forestalled any remark by saying, "With your permission, Mr. President, I will keep these on, otherwise it would be embarrassing if we should meet ladies." And so we jumped into the water and swam across.[1]

Thayer ended his story by noting that Jusserand earned the respect of Roosevelt that day, and the two became lifelong friends. If there was anything Roosevelt admired, it was a man who fully embraced his masculinity.

But there was much more to Theodore Roosevelt than determination and hardiness. Writer Edwyn Sandys described the new American president as individual in the best sense of the word:

Had Roosevelt never set eyes upon the White House, he still would have been famous. Had he never aspired to be more than an American country gentleman with a passion for wild sport and an ability to write useful books, his name would have been widely known, for he has the power of impressing his individuality upon whatever he does, and that individuality ever is the stamp of a vigorous, fearless, observant and kindly man.[2]

Theodore Roosevelt was indeed a remarkable, though imperfect human being. To modern readers, he's even something of a contradiction. He was a conservationist who enjoyed hunting, a man with a strong sense of justice who encouraged violent revolution in Panama, and a gentle family man who was at times downright vicious to his political opponents. In a sense, though, it is precisely these paradoxes that continue to make Theodore Roosevelt seem larger than life. While a lesser man may have been hamstrung by his failings, Roosevelt was able to rise above them often enough to positively alter the course of a nation.

~

IN 1858, when Theodore Roosevelt was born, the United States had a population of nearly thirty million people scattered across thirty-two states. It was a young nation; less than a hundred years had passed since the signing of the Declaration of Independence and the ratification of the Constitution. James Madison, the last of the Founding Fathers, had died only a generation earlier, in 1836. Some Americans alive at the time had grandparents and parents who had fought in the Revolutionary War and the War of 1812.

In the 1800s, the United States was slowly stepping out of the economic and cultural shadow of traditional European powers like Great Britain, France, and Germany and was on the way to becoming a world power in its own right. The Industrial Revolution that came in the 1820s and 30s had led to a rapid transformation of American life. Between 1790 and 1850, the population rose over 500 percent, and many heeded the call to "Go West, young man" with unbridled exuberance. By mid-century, the nation had fulfilled its "manifest destiny," stretching from the established states of the East, on through the prairies of the Midwest, and clear across to the Pacific. By 1853, there were already plans in motion to build a railroad traversing the 3,000–plus miles, from sea to shining sea.

America in the 1850s was a nation on the move, but it still had to face the unresolved business of slavery. Many leading Americans recognized that the bald statement of the Declaration of Independence that "all men are created equal" was inconsistent with the existence of slavery.[3] On October 15, 1858, just two weeks before Theodore Roosevelt was born, Abraham Lincoln said in a debate with Stephen A. Douglas, "[T]he fathers of this government expected and intended the institution of slavery to come to an end."[4]

Politicians from both North and South searched in vain for a resolution to the issue that would not tear the nation in two, but in the end none was forthcoming. Lincoln was proved correct in his belief that "a house divided cannot stand." To settle the issue of slavery, America would have to pass the severe testing of a four-year civil war, one that almost brought an end to its grand experiment in freedom and democracy. No Americans, not even the privileged Roosevelt family, were untouched. Hundreds of thousands lost their lives.

As the Civil War was coming to an end, and a Union victory was assured, discussion turned to how the secessionist Confederate states would be brought back into the Union. President Lincoln wanted this done with relative ease, but after he was assassinated, the so-called Radical Republicans in Congress took control of the process. They rewrote southern state constitutions, and they sent federal troops into the South until 1877. Combined with destroyed crops and ravaged cities, this set the economic recovery of the South back by decades.

Outside of the South, the end of the war brought with it an economic renaissance. Racial problems persisted, but there was a feeling of unbounded optimism, which was strengthened even more by notable achievements. On May 10, 1869, the final piece of the Transcontinental Railroad was set in place, uniting America by rail. Homesteaders rushed westward to claim inexpensive tracts of land as businessmen sought fortunes in mining, lumber, and salmon fishing. The invention of the elevator led to a boom in the construction of skyscrapers, and in the 1870s the typewriter brought women into the workplace. Not surprisingly, the first rags-to-riches Horatio Alger novel, *Ragged Dick*, was published in 1867 to almost instant success.

In many cities restaurants created lunch counters to serve meals of roast beef and coffee to quick-moving businessmen who couldn't spare the time for a leisurely meal. The world seemed to be changing at a dizzying pace. By 1900, a full 40 percent of Americans were living in urban areas, and one-third were first or second generation Americans. For those who craved a sense of community often lacking in the big city, organizations such as the Rotary Club, as well as neighborhood bars, offered a small-town feeling.

By most socioeconomic standards, the United States in the second half of the nineteenth century was the envy of the world. In 1860, it was the world's fourth largest manufacturer; by 1894, it was first. By the 1870s, Russian Mennonites brought hearty winter wheat, a variety that could be harvested in the spring before the arrival of destructive locusts, to the plains of Kansas. Soon railroads were carrying it to America's tables.

A bevy of remarkable inventions were made, and through mass production they quickly went from exclusive playthings of the rich to staples of middle-class life. Due to the business savvy of Sears and Roebuck and Montgomery Ward and others, more and more Americans enjoyed such things as sewing machines, chewing gum, Vaseline, telephones, phonographs, incandescent electric lights, vacuum cleaners, roller skates, curling irons, Hires root beer, and bottled ketchup. A pre-automotive bicycle craze swept America, with four million riders on the roads by 1896. Newspapers proliferated, itinerant photographers began capturing American life on film, and P.T. Barnum's circus used the railroads to reach millions with "the Greatest Show on Earth." Industrialist-turned-philanthropist Andrew Carnegie summed up the American economic boom: "The old nations of the earth creep at a snail's pace. The Republic thunders past with the rush of an express."[5]

America wasn't without its growing pains, however. In the postwar years, slavery had been replaced by Jim Crow laws that prevented many blacks in the South from exercising their right to vote. Others on the edges of society were left behind as the economy steamed forward into the twentieth century. Immigrants from all over Europe were flooding into the nation, and many lacked the skills necessary to succeed in America without a helping hand.

By the time the United States entered World War I in 1917, a nation of shopkeepers had become both an economic and a military powerhouse. Theodore Roosevelt, president for most of the twentieth century's first decade, could claim a share of the credit for this amazing national makeover. Roosevelt was not deaf to the cries of the poor and the oppressed, first in New York and then across the country, and he sought solutions that would allow as many Americans as possible to participate in the nation's prosperity. Using the White House as a "bully pulpit," President Roosevelt argued that America was a nation of destiny, and he set out to prove it.

CHAPTER ONE

New Birth

IN 1644, when Klaes Martensen van Rosenvelt—whose name in Dutch meant "field of roses"—left his rose fields in Holland and hitched a ride on a sailing ship to the New World, he could never have imagined that his family would one day become one of the wealthiest and most influential in America. Rosenvelt arrived in the Dutch colony of New Amsterdam, which was later renamed New York when the territory came under British control. When Rosenvelt disembarked, he took his place within "a cosmopolitan town of four hundred or five hundred inhabitants who spoke eighteen different languages."[1] Soon the family, who changed their name to Roosevelt, became successful merchants and traders.

In America, the Roosevelts married people of Scottish, Irish, Welsh, Huguenot French, and German ancestry, leading some to nickname their descendant Theodore "Old Fifty-Seven Varieties" when he campaigned for office in the 1880s. His maternal great-great-grandfather, Archibald Bulloch, was a member of the Continental Congress and the first state governor of Georgia. Theodore's paternal great-grandfather, James, along with other family members, served in the Continental Army against the British during the Revolutionary War. After the war ended, James Roosevelt opened a successful hardware store with his son, Cornelius, which operated until 1824 in New York City.

When James died, Cornelius van Schaack Roosevelt inherited his father's fortune and invested much of it in businesses and real estate. Cornelius also ran a highly profitable glass importing business, and he gradually became one of wealthiest men in New York. His son, Theodore Roosevelt Sr., was known as "Thee" to family and friends. He married Martha "Mittie" Bulloch, who was from an affluent family in Georgia, on December 22, 1853. They lived on East Twentieth Street in New York City in a newly constructed brownstone home that was a wedding gift from Cornelius.

Although he had considerable wealth, Thee Roosevelt never liked to talk about money. An unfailingly compassionate man, he believed that it was his duty as a Christian and as a gentleman to do all he could to help the less fortunate. And in the boiling cauldron of New York City, there were many—from new immigrants to homeless children— who desperately needed a helping hand. A whole spate of religious and secular groups, many founded or supported by Thee Roosevelt, arose to meet the need for compassion.

At the time, it was believed that private citizens and organizations, not federal or state governments, had the primary responsibility to care for the less fortunate. Later, when Thee's son, Theodore Roosevelt Jr., became involved in politics, however, he pushed for a much more proactive governmental role in combating poverty and other forms of injustice. The younger Theodore "had a sharp contempt for the 'idle rich' and strong convictions on the duty of the leisure class to the community."[2]

Thee Roosevelt was a tireless advocate for the indigent citizens of New York. He was involved with the Young Men's Christian Association (YMCA) from its earliest days, and he helped begin the New York Orthopedic Hospital. He supported Miss Slattery's Night School for Little Italians, and he also managed to convince his wealthy friends to support the Newsboys' Lodging House, a residence for the homeless and neglected children who hawked the city's daily newspapers. Thee was a man without a trace of snobbery, and he mixed willingly and easily with rich and poor alike.

As a young man, Theodore Roosevelt remembered his father taking him and his siblings to visit the Newsboys' Lodging House so that they would always remember their responsibility to others. From an early age, Theodore saw that wealth and privilege could—and should—be used to help others in need. Later in his life, when Roosevelt believed that rich and powerful business interests were grinding the poor and working classes into the dust, he used his political clout to help protect the civil and economic rights of the underprivileged. Always, however, he wished more for the poor than a lifetime of poverty.

$\sim$

IN 1858, when Theodore Roosevelt was born, New York was a city of sharp contrasts. The magazine *Harper's Weekly* described it as "a huge semi-barbarous metropolis . . . not well-governed nor ill-governed, but simply not governed at all—filthy and unlighted streets—no practical or efficient security for either life of property—a police not worthy of the name—and expenses steadily and enormously increasing."[3] An average of 235,000 immigrants came through the port of New York annually. While many were headed for points north, west, and south, a good number stayed in New York itself, swelling the population. At nearly one million people (including sister city Brooklyn), New York was far and away the nation's largest city, and one-third of its residents had arrived from overseas in the previous ten years.

The city struggled to provide for the newcomers, and not always successfully. Thomas Jefferson had warned in 1787, "When we get piled upon one another in large cities, we shall become as corrupt as Europe, and go on eating one another as they do there."[4] The truth of his words was manifest. By 1865, an estimated 100,000 New Yorkers lived in slums, tenement homes where poverty, crime, prostitution, and diseases like cholera and malaria were commonplace. One especially notorious section of Manhattan was the Five Points neighborhood, which the *New York Tribune* in 1849 called "the great central ulcer of wretchedness." Large families of mainly Irish immigrants squeezed into cramped and dingy apartments, while many more slept on streets filled with orphaned child laborers, prostitutes, drunks, and thieves. All were forced to cope with piles of rotting garbage that often were three feet deep. In 1857, and again in 1863, the largely foreign-born inhabitants of Five Points had rioted, terrifying their far wealthier neighbors in uptown Manhattan. By 1900, there were 42,700 tenement buildings in Manhattan, and they provided housing for 1.5 million residents.

Elsewhere in Manhattan, urban architects were making plans for a public park to rival those that wealthy New Yorkers had seen in London and Paris. In 1853, the state legislature had acquired 700 acres of land in central Manhattan, and in the winter of 1858 the first part of the new Central Park designed by Frederick Law Olmstead was opened to the public. Affluent New Yorkers skated on the park's twenty-acre lake for the first time, and as many as ten thousand skaters were on the ice at one time. *Harper's Weekly* praised the park as a "sylvan miracle, teeming with bowers of romantic liveliness and dripping with fountains of the clearest crystal."[5] During the milder months, horses and buggies took fashionable New Yorkers for pleasant drives around the park's greenery. Because it was not within walking distance of working-class neighborhoods, Central Park was the nearly exclusive domain of the wealthy until the 1920s.

~

THEODORE WAS BORN a few days before his mother's due date. On the evening of October 27, 1858, soon after his mother had returned from a last-minute shopping trip, Theodore Roosevelt Jr., was born into wealth and privilege on the second floor of the family home in New York City. His grandmother, Martha Stewart Bulloch, who was present at his birth, said that Theodore was "as sweet and pretty a young baby as I have ever seen."[6] He weighed over eight pounds and was described as a bright and happy child. By ten months, he had acquired the nickname "Teedie."

Before he was three years old, however, Theodore began to develop severe asthma and had great difficulty breathing. He was sick as a child just like his older sister, Anna (known to friends and family as "Bamie"), who was born in 1855 with a spinal deformity known as Pott's disease. Theodore often had to sleep propped up in bed or in a chair, and his parents did all they could to help him. They gave him strong black coffee and nicotine from a cigar, which were common treatments at the time, and took him for trips to the country, the seashore, and the mountains for the fresh air. His father would sometimes take Teedie on brisk carriage rides around the neighborhood to force air into his lungs. Nothing would work for very long, and soon his asthma would return.

Physically, Theodore was pale, with unruly hair, large teeth, and nearsighted blue eyes. Like other sick children, he loved to read, especially adventure stories about the American frontier. At an early age, these stories, combined with his father's example, helped Theodore form ideas and opinions about masculinity that would remain with him throughout his life.

"As a small boy," he remembered, "I had *Our Young Folks*, which I then firmly believed to be the very best magazine in the world. . . . 'Cast Away in the Cold,' 'Grandfather's Struggle for a Homestead' . . . and a dozen others like them were first-class, good healthy stories, interesting in the first place, and in the next place teaching manliness, decency, and good conduct."[7] He also read classics such as *Swiss Family Robinson*, *Little Men*, *Little Women*, and *Robinson Crusoe*. According to his sister, Corinne,

> My earliest impressions of my brother Theodore are those of a rather small, patient, suffering little child, who, in spite of suffering, was always acknowledged head of the nursery . . . where my brother Elliot[t] and I were his loving followers in any game which he initiated, or where we listened with intense interest and admiration to the stories which he wove for us day by day, and often even month by month.[8]

Theodore was the second of four children born to Thee and Mittie Roosevelt. Anna ("Bamie") was the oldest, and after Theodore were Elliott ("Ellie") born in 1860, and Corinne ("Conie") born in 1861. The four children became good friends, even though Theodore, Elliott, and Corinne were closest by virtue of their age. Theodore was all boy, despite his fragile health. An early biographer tells the story of one time when Roosevelt was four and earned "his first and only spanking":

> For some reason or other not quite clear he had bitten his sister's arm. This was a crime, he knew, and he fled forthwith to the backyard and thence to the kitchen, where the cook, who was Irish, was baking bread. He seized a handful of dough (preparedness!) and crawled under the kitchen table. A minute later his father entered from the yard, asking for Theodore. The cook was warm-hearted, and compromised between "informing" and her conscience by casting a significant glance under the table. The elder Theodore Roosevelt dropped on all-fours and darted for the younger. That fugitive from justice heaved the dough at him and bolted for the stairway. He was caught half-way up and treated on the whole as he deserved.[9]

Despite this indiscretion, and surely others not recorded for posterity, Theodore and his sisters remained close even as they became adults. While Elliott drifted into alcoholism and became estranged from his family, Anna and Corinne adored their brother, and he made sure to write to them whenever he was away from New York.

≈

THREE YEARS AFTER Theodore was born, the nation was plunged into a Civil War, which lasted for four long years. His father supported Abraham Lincoln and the Union, but Theodore's mother and her family in Georgia supported the Confederate cause. Thee wanted to enlist in the Union army, but he didn't want to anger his wife, so instead he helped to get financial assistance to the families of Union soldiers. Like many other wealthy men, Thee paid a substitute to fight in his place on

Young "Teedy" at age four. *Theodore Roosevelt Collection, Harvard College Library*

the field of battle. Later he would begin to feel a real and profound sense of guilt about this.

The administration of the war enabled Thee to become close friends with the Lincolns, and when Abraham Lincoln was assassinated, the Roosevelt family shared in the nation's grief. On Tuesday afternoon, June 25, 1865, a fourteen-foot-long funeral car drawn by sixteen horses and bearing the body of the murdered president passed in front of Cornelius Roosevelt's home in New York City. Watching from a second-floor window (which easily could have been rented for $100 per person that day) was six-year-old Theodore Roosevelt and his brother, Elliott. Their playmate Edith Carow was also there, but she was so overcome by grief that Theodore and Elliott put her in another room to quiet her down. The sight of 75,000 people marching in procession with Lincoln's coffin made a lasting impression on the future president; as an adult, he would dedicate most of his life to advancing the Republican ideals Lincoln espoused.

Theodore was a very curious little boy, and a lifelong fascination with nature came early on in his childhood. Before he could even read, he found a copy of African explorer and anti-slavery activist Dr. David Livingstone's *Missionary Travels and Researches in Southern Africa* in the family library. The pictures of the birds and animals were captivating, and he asked Bamie and his mother to read the book to him.

When he was seven, Theodore noticed a dead seal on display at an outdoor market near his home. He went back to view the seal again and again, studying the carcass and measuring it. When the seal was finally taken away, the boy was given the skull. This was the beginning of the "Roosevelt Museum of Natural History," a collection of preserved animals that grew over the years as Theodore added more specimens.

Young Theodore filled notebooks with descriptions of animals he found, and he even begged his mother to bring back feathers from one of her trips. He collected frogs, snakes, mice, and other animals from his neighborhood, adding many to the Roosevelt Museum of Natural History. (Much to his mother's chagrin, some of his specimens ended up in the icebox!) When he was nine, he wrote a treatise entitled "Natural History of Insects." Years later, as an avid hunter and conservationist, Roosevelt remembered warmly that his parents encouraged his interest in nature, "as they always did in anything that could give me wholesome pleasure or help develop me."[10]

Like other children of wealthy families at that time, Theodore was taught at home. His aunt, Anna Bulloch, taught him his numbers, how to read and write, and told him exciting stories of his relatives who fought in the American Revolution. He never became a good speller, though, and he was poor at math.

But health problems continued to cast a long shadow over the young boy's life. By the time he was ten years old, Theodore's asthma showed few signs of improvement. In an effort to help, the Roosevelt family left for a year-long trip to Europe in May 1869. Beginning in England, the family journeyed to Scotland, France, Switzerland, Germany, and Italy. During the trip, Theodore and his father exercised by walking twenty miles a day, but Theodore's asthma continued to be a problem. At one point, he couldn't muster enough wind to blow out a candle.

CHAPTER TWO

Mind and Body

THEE ROOSEVELT loved his son and knew the time had come to give him a bit of fatherly encouragement. Soon after the family arrived back in New York from Europe in May 1870, he took Theodore aside. "Theodore," he said, "you have the mind but not the body, and without the help of the body the mind cannot go as far as it should. You must make your body. It is hard drudgery to make one's body but I know you will do it."[1]

Theodore loved his father, who was the embodiment of the "real man" Theodore wanted to become as an adult. If his father thought that physical strength would help him become more of a man, then that was all the motivation Theodore needed. According to his sister, Corinne, Theodore looked up at their father and smiled, then said with enthusiasm, "I'll make my body!"[2]

His mother took the boy to a gymnasium operated by John Wood, where Theodore immediately began working out on chest exercise machines. Wood believed, not without justification, that strengthening Theodore's chest muscles would help him breathe better. After a short time, Thee was so satisfied with Theodore's progress that he had Wood set up a private gym in the open-air porch on the second floor of the family's home.

In what would become his characteristic approach to life, Theodore went full steam ahead with his strength-training routine.

Over the next few years, he spent much of his free time in the family gym, swinging on bars, punching a bag, and working out with weights. His health improved so much that in August 1871 he was well enough to go on a family camping trip. Theodore had a grand time sleeping on the ground, shooting the surging water of the river rapids in a canoe, and climbing mountains. And for one of the first times in his life, he didn't have an asthma attack for an entire month.

Once home, the boy jumped back into his scientific activities. He studied taxidermy and went hunting in the wilderness areas of Long Island. Later he recalled that he wasn't a good shot and could never manage to hit much. The reason, he found, was that his eyesight was poor. Once he was fitted with glasses, his aim—as well as the size of the Roosevelt Museum of Natural History collection—improved dramatically.

Hunting would always play an important role in Theodore Roosevelt's life. Friends suggested that the plethora of hunting trophies on display at Roosevelt's adult home at Sagamore Hill was a visible symbol of Theodore's ability to overcome the limitations of illness and, in a sense, the perceived unmanliness of wealth, to become a "real man." As his friend, Hermann Hagedorn, would later write:

> Theodore took more pride in those game-heads than in any of the books he had written or the political achievements that had already carried his name across the continent. They meant manhood to him, manhood won at a price: tokens of triumph of character over physical inadequacy, testimony to daring, strength, endurance, straight aim and steady nerves, none of them innate, all laboriously acquired.[3]

THEODORE'S GRANDFATHER, Cornelius, died in 1871, and he left Thee and his brother each more than $1 million. This was an enormous sum of money, considering that the average American family earned about $500 a year at the time. The financial windfall meant that Thee could finally move out of the family importing business and focus on his two real loves: family and philanthropy.

Thee's new wealth helped convince him to sell the family home on Twentieth Street, which was an ever-present reminder of his father. He financed the building of a larger house on West Fifty-seventh Street, which was a country setting at the time and just off Fifth Avenue, near Central Park. The house was also next door to that of his brother, James, who had established the Roosevelt family in investment banking and real estate.

◁∼▷

WHILE THEIR NEW house was being constructed, toward the end of 1872, the Roosevelt family went on a second overseas adventure. The highlight of the trip was a two-month cruise up the Nile River in a houseboat Thee had rented for the then-extraordinary sum of $2,000. During their journey, the Roosevelts met the writer Ralph Waldo Emerson and his daughter, who were touring Egypt at the time. Theodore also saw dozens of beautiful birds along the Nile, and he killed and stuffed nearly two hundred of them.

The Roosevelts went on to the Holy Land, Beirut, Damascus, Constantinople, Athens, and finally Vienna. Theodore's asthma had been absent during the two months the family was in Egypt, which was the longest period of his life to that point. When they moved on to the colder countries of Europe, though, his asthma returned.

In May 1873, while their father was on business in Vienna, Theodore, Elliott, and Corinne were sent to live for a few months with the Minkwitz family in Dresden, Germany. There Theodore learned German well and developed a love of the German people that lasted until the years leading up to World War I. During his stay, Theodore continued to pursue his science. His love of nature had increased with each year, and he began to talk about a career as a professional scientist. He sometimes frightened members of the Minkwitz family with the bats and other species he brought into their house. Theodore's other passion, a love of the written word, was more acceptable; Theodore and a few other American children formed the Dresden

Literary American Club, and met on Sunday afternoons to read the poetry and stories of its members.

In spite of these pleasures, Theodore's summer in Germany was not completely enjoyable. He was sick with the mumps, he suffered from headaches, and he was attacked by increasingly intense bouts of asthma. When the Roosevelts left Dresden, Theodore's mother told Anna Minkwitz that she was worried about her son's future. Anna replied, "You need not be anxious about him. He will surely one day be a great professor, or who knows, he may become even President of the United States."[4]

In the fall of 1873, the Roosevelts moved into their new home in New York City. It had Persian carpets on the floors, mirrors and crystal in the ballroom, and ornate hand-carved woodwork throughout the house. The attic contained the ever-expanding Roosevelt Museum of Natural History, and the top floor housed a gymnasium for Theodore. Despite the three-year financial panic that began in September and led to over 23,000 business failures, the Roosevelt fortune, centered as it was on property, remained secure.

This was the family's winter home. Thee Roosevelt also joined his relatives at Oyster Bay in Long Island by renting a summer house there, some forty miles from the city. Cousins and friends frequently overran it. The children sailed and rowed on the bay or Long Island Sound, and they also hunted and explored the woods on foot and horseback. For a young outdoorsman like Theodore Roosevelt, it must have felt like heaven on earth.

During these adolescent years, Theodore faced some ridicule from other boys, who called him "four-eyes" because of his glasses, but he did everything in his power to charm the young ladies by taking on the role of explorer and language expert. At times it seemed to work. He picnicked with Annie Murray, rowed in the moonlight with Nellie Smith, and went riding with Fanny Smith. At other times, however, Roosevelt had less success with the fairer sex, which may have been due less to his personality and more to his infrequent bathing, even after he had been handling the preservative arsenic and dead animals in his taxidermy.

In New York, he attended dance class with Edith Carow, his favorite companion at this time. It seems that she wanted more out of the relationship, but Theodore apparently wasn't entertaining any such ideas. He did admit, however, that she was pretty, well-dressed, and "the most cultivated, best-read girl I know."[5] But Edith's charms, such as they were, apparently couldn't compensate for the dancing classes themselves. Theodore lamented to his aunt, "We have to go to dancing school. I do not like it much."[6]

IN 1874, when Theodore was sixteen, he joined St. Nicholas Dutch Reformed Church, and he was a member until the time of his death. Also that year, his father decided to enroll him at Harvard College in the fall of 1876. But before Theodore could join the Ivy League, he would first need to pass the university's difficult entrance exams. For others who had attended school on a regular basis this might not have posed a great problem, but Theodore's home-school education was spotty at best. As he later recalled, "I could not go to school [Harvard] because I knew so much less than most boys of my age in some subjects and so much more in others. In science and history and geography and in unexpected parts of German and French I was strong, but lamentably weak in Latin and Greek and mathematics."[7]

Theodore had two years to prepare for the entrance exams, but he would need every second of that time. Because Theodore's health had declined somewhat, Thee decided that his son should get intensive tutoring at home instead of being sent away to boarding school.

The man Thee selected to prepare Theodore for the Harvard exams was Arthur Cutler, a talented young Harvard graduate who later founded a prestigious school in New York and even later was an honored guest at the Roosevelt White House. Cutler marveled at "the alert, vigorous character of young Roosevelt's mind,"[8] and the two

Theodore as a freshman at Harvard, ready to take on the world. *Theodore Roosevelt Collection, Harvard College Library*

quickly became friends as they focused on filling in the gaps in the boy's knowledge. They worked eight hours a day, and they managed to cover three years' worth of material in only two years.

Characteristically, Theodore was in a state of almost perpetual motion. Cutler later wrote, "The young man never seemed to know what idleness was."[9] When not reading a novel or a scientific treatise, he was adding specimens to the Roosevelt Museum of Natural History.

He still had every intention of becoming a professional scientist—at the time, a gentleman and a naturalist, not a laboratory researcher in a white coat. His passion for the subject was strong. "Along with my college preparatory studies," he wrote later,

> I carried on the work of a practical student of natural history. I worked with greater industry than either intelligence or success, and made very few additions to the sum of human knowledge; but to this day certain obscure ornithological publications may be found in which are recorded such items as, for instance, that on one occasion a fish-crow, and on another an Ipswich sparrow, were obtained by one Theodore Roosevelt, Jr., at Oyster Bay, on the shore of Long Island Sound.[10]

When it came time for his preliminary Harvard exams in 1875, Theodore passed them easily. "Is it not splendid about my examinations?" he exclaimed. "I passed well on all the eight subjects I tried."[11]

By the following summer, Theodore was accepted into the Harvard class of 1880. Adding to that good news was the fact that his asthma seemed to be under control for the first time in his life. After years of physical exercise, he was healthier than ever, although with a 26 1/2-inch waist he was still skinny. He was tanned from a summer of rowing at Oyster Bay, and he had grown long, fashionable sideburns to bring out his powerful jaw line.

That summer, a time of nationwide celebrations of America's one-hundredth birthday, was one of the happiest of Theodore's life. Now that he had achieved his goal, he had time to relax. His interest in girls seems to have been rekindled in the process. Although the details are somewhat murky, Theodore's relationship with Edith Carow began to move beyond mere friendship, and one of his boating excursions was to her family's summer home. Years later, family members suggested that Theodore and Edith had planned on getting married.

It was also Thee Roosevelt's last chance to give Theodore some advice. Thee, who had never gone to college, talked at length with his son about the future. While he and the rest of the family hoped

Theodore would choose a legal or business career, Theodore insisted that he would become a scientist, despite the fact that it was seen as a profession far less suitable to a man of his upbringing. In a letter written to Theodore a few days before his departure for Harvard College, Thee advised his son to look after his morals, his health, and his studies—in that order. On September 27, as the train slowly pulled away from the Syosset, Long Island, railroad station and headed west for New York City, it took with it a young man determined to make his father proud.

CHAPTER THREE

Phoenix Rising

THEODORE DIDN'T LIVE in the freshman dorms, as most Harvard freshmen did. He feared that the dampness of those ground floor apartments would cause his asthma to flare up again. He also needed space for the animal specimens he hoped to collect, and he was sure they wouldn't be welcome in a campus dorm.

His older sister, Bamie, was sent to Cambridge, Massachusetts, ahead of Theodore to find him a place to live. Bamie chose and furnished a comfortable apartment at 16 Winthrop Street, on the second floor of a house a few blocks from campus. She made sure to bring Theodore's stuffed birds—and over the next four years Theodore would add live snakes, salamanders, lobsters, and a large tortoise. The rooms had four windows and a fireplace that was lit by a manservant every morning. A woman was hired to do his laundry.

When Theodore arrived at Harvard, the college was very much a destination for the children of powerful white Protestant families. There were 821 students, and Theodore joined a freshman class of 246 men. None of them were foreigners, blacks, Boston Irish, Jewish, or women. There was a sense of community, however. As one writer noted, "You belonged to Harvard, and she to you."[1]

In such a privileged and homogeneous environment, most students had a similar understanding of the world, and many cultivated indifference toward the events beyond the college's ivy-coated walls. It wasn't surprising, then, that Theodore's intense interest in the wider world initially led to trouble with his fellow classmates. They called him "Roosevelt of New York," and noted that he wore thick eyeglasses and had a high-pitched voice. Sometimes Theodore's mind was working so quickly that his mouth couldn't keep up, and some of what he said came across as gibberish. Those who knew him described him as "eccentric" or even "half-crazy."

Theodore did go on to make several good friends at Harvard, but partly because of how he appeared to his classmates he was not wildly popular. Theodore also took a snobbish attitude toward his classmates, considering only a few to be well-mannered gentlemen worthy of his friendship. The young man's personality, which would help him in navigating treacherous political waters in later years, was very much on display at this time. While most students felt it proper to walk around campus with the casual, characteristic Harvard "swing," Theodore literally ran. And while many of his classmates took pride in being dispassionate—a popular student poem was entitled "Ode to Indifference"—Theodore loved to argue and exhort about anything that interested him, which classmates and professors sensed was nearly everything.

In class, he frequently interrupted professors with questions. One couldn't take it any longer and snorted, "See here, Roosevelt, let me talk. I'm running this course."[2] Theodore was also able to focus on something so intently that he didn't pay attention to anyone or anything else. One story told about him is that he was so absorbed in a book he was reading before the fireplace in his room that he only knew his boots were on fire when he smelled them burning.

Exuberance did not equal wildness, however. Theodore was a very disciplined student. He woke up at 7:15 for mandatory chapel services at 7:45, had breakfast, went to class until noon, had lunch, studied for an hour, then went to class for another hour. He had free time from 3:30 until dinner at 6, then spent the evening studying, having visitors, and reading and writing until he went to bed around 11 o'clock. For his afternoon exercise, he walked, boxed, and rowed on the Charles River near campus. On Saturdays, Theodore studied for six hours.

Although he was a member of the Dutch Reformed Church, Theodore taught a Sunday school class at Christ Episcopal Church in Cambridge. His early biographer Thayer noted that Theodore "was so muscular a Christian that the decorous vestrymen thought him an unwise guide to piety." In one case, Theodore congratulated a brother who got a black eye from fighting a larger boy who had pinched his sister "and gave him a dollar as a reward. The vestrymen decided that this was too flagrant [an] approval of fisticuffs; so the young teacher soon found a welcome in the Sunday School of a different denomination."[3] In his senior year, Theodore taught a mission class at a church in East Cambridge.

It was at Harvard that Theodore began to transform himself from a scruffy scientist who smelled like formaldehyde and arsenic into a dandy who was terribly interested in appearances. He began to join exclusive Harvard clubs, have tea and opera parties, and dress in fashionable English-cut suits. He also began to part his hair in the middle. A pocket watch, walking stick, and a beaver hat rounded out his new look.

As a rising member of the privileged class, Theodore had his share of social obligations. He attended numerous dinner parties, dances, and suppers in Boston, Milton, and Cambridge. To improve his dancing ability, Theodore took lessons, but one woman who knew him said he was hardly a born dancer. He also enjoyed ice skating and co-ed sleigh rides in the cold Massachusetts winters. Though he apparently attracted the interest of other young women, Theodore affirmed his devotion to Edith.

∽

ROOSEVELT WASN'T overly involved in politics during his college years. Like most members of the upper class, he was a Republican, as was his father before him. The wealthy believed that the Republican Party would work to maintain an atmosphere in which talented men could achieve success in the business world. The Democrats, on the other hand, were largely seen by the rich as a party of revolutionaries who wanted to overturn the social order and introduce a socialist system whereby wealth would be redistributed to the unproductive members of society, to the detriment of all.

Roosevelt initially held the common upperclass view that politics was a business filled with liars and cheats—not a suitable career for a gentleman. When he first arrived at Harvard, though, he may have participated in a parade supporting Republican presidential candidate Rutherford B. Hayes. Hayes campaigned on a promise to reduce government corruption by reforming the civil service, and many Harvard students joined others across the nation in chanting, "Hurrah for Hayes and Honest Ways!!" Roosevelt was also enamored with Hayes, whose uncompromising integrity may have reminded the young man of his father. There is a story that the freshman Roosevelt cheered so loudly for Hayes during a student rally in October 1876 that an upperclassman threw a potato at him from a second-story window.

The choice of Hayes by a single electoral college vote in the disputed election of 1876 drew Theodore's father—again reluctantly—into politics. Convinced of Hayes's good intentions, in late 1877 Thee accepted the nomination for a position as a collector of customs in New York. Although most members of his social class regarded politics as a "dirty business" conducted by lower class professional politicians out to line their own pockets, Thee Roosevelt believed that it was time to return the running of government to those he called the "best men."

He ran into considerable opposition, however. Powerful interests who profited from government corruption lobbied against him, and the Senate narrowly rejected his nomination. The political infighting surrounding Thee's nomination took its toll on a dignified and honest man not used to the rough-and-tumble world of politics. His health began to suffer, and he died of stomach cancer on February 9, 1878. He was forty-six years old. As a testament to his untiring work for the less fortunate of New York, flags around the city flew at half-mast in his honor.

Theodore took the loss very hard. In some ways he would never be the same again. "Sometimes," he wrote in his diary, "when I think of my terrible loss it seems as if my heart would break; he shared all my joys, and in sharing doubled them, and soothed all the sorrows I ever had."[4] Theodore was so saddened by the loss of his father that once, while attending the family's church at Oyster Bay, he was convinced he'd seen his father. "I could see him sitting in the corner of the [church] pew as distinctly as if he were alive, in the same dear old attitude. . . . Oh, I feel so sad when I think of the word 'never.'"[5]

His father had left Theodore $125,000 in his will, but the money seemed unimportant. What mattered was that the center of Theodore's universe had been taken from him. To help cope with his grief, Theodore finally resolved to "study well" and to be "like a brave Christian gentleman,"[6] but it could not have been easy. Like others before and since, the tragedy led Theodore to a period of spiritual reflection, and a year after his father's death he wrote, "Nothing but my faith in the Lord Jesus Christ could have carried me through this, my terrible time of trial and sorrow."[7]

That summer he spent time with Edith at Oyster Bay, and her emotional support throughout such a wrenching time must have been invaluable to Theodore. Indeed, as he began to contemplate life without his father, Theodore may have felt the time was right to go resolutely forward—with Edith by his side. Family members later said that Theodore had asked Edith to marry him that difficult summer, but she had refused. Perhaps she knew that he wasn't in any condition to make life-altering decisions. Years later, Theodore confessed to Bamie, "[Edith] and I had very intimate relations; one day there came a break for we both of us had, and I suppose have, tempers that were far from being of the best. To no soul now living have either of us ever since spoken a word of this."[8]

CHAPTER FOUR

"My Own Sweet, Pretty Darling"

WHEN FALL CAME, Theodore returned to Harvard for his junior year. He had determined to cover his sorrow with his schoolwork. He took a hefty load of nine courses, including electives in German, zoology, and geology. His hard work paid off, and by the end of the year he had averaged a grade of eighty-seven, the highest he would ever receive at Harvard.

As he was plowing through his coursework, Theodore could not have known that Cupid's arrow, in the form of a young woman, was about to pierce his heart. Her name was Alice Lee, and she would be the salve that helped to heal the wounds left by Thee's death.

Theodore Roosevelt and Alice Lee met at the Chestnut Hill home of Richard Saltonstall, one of Theodore's closest friends and a fellow member of several exclusive Harvard clubs. The date was Friday, October 18. Alice was Richard's cousin and nextdoor neighbor, a girl who could trace her ancestry back to the original settlers from the *Mayflower* in 1620. Her father was a well-connected Boston banker. By all accounts, she was a beauty—a tall, gray-eyed, seventeen-year-old with curly light brown hair—the best friend of Richard's sister, Rose. She was blessed with a warm personality and a quick wit; her nickname was "Sunshine."

When Theodore first noticed Alice, he soon forgot about any romantic entanglements with Edith Carow: "As long as I live, I shall never forget how sweetly she looked, and how prettily she greeted me."[1] He gushed that was "beautiful in face and form, and lovelier still in spirit."[2]

Although Theodore fell deeply in love with Alice, she still took some convincing before she fell in love with Theodore, whom she called "Teddy." With his thick glasses, energy, and determined attitude, he wasn't her idea of a proper husband. She was a little intimidated by his overbearing personality, and she especially disliked Theodore telling her about the variety of wild animals he kept in his apartment.

Theodore set out to win Alice's heart. It was almost literally true that he was with Alice whenever he wasn't at Harvard. In winter, they went ice skating and took sleigh rides, and they read to one another before the fire. In spring, Theodore rode his horse to Chestnut Hill almost daily, and the couple played tennis and went sailing and horseback riding together. Not holding anything back, he even befriended Alice's five-year-old brother by telling him thrilling stories about wolves and bears. Many long remembered Theodore pointing to Alice at a party and saying to a friend, "See that girl? I am going to marry her. She won't have me, but I am going to have *her*!"[3]

Theodore was deeply in love, and he said later that Alice was "always present" in his mind. Over time, his persistence paid off and Alice warmed to him. Theodore was unlike any man she had ever met. Certainly he was more colorful than the starchy sons of wealth and power that she had known for most of her young life.

Finally, on January 25, 1880, with Alice's defenses successfully circumvented, Theodore proposed. The sheer force of his personality made him a hard man to turn down. He wrote, "after much pleading, my own sweet, pretty darling consented to be my wife . . . How she, so pure and sweet and beautiful can think of marrying me I cannot understand, but I praise and thank God it is so."[4]

For her part, Alice was excited to be engaged, but her enthusiasm was somewhat subdued. Perhaps she was weary from Theodore's dogged pursuit. Still, she wrote to his mother about "feeling so unworthy of such a noble man's love. But I do love Theodore deeply and it

Alice Lee, Theodore's first wife, was "beautiful in face and form, and lovelier still in spirit." *Library of Congress*

will be my aim both to endear myself to those dear to him and retain his love. How happy I am I can't begin to tell you, it seems almost like a dream."[5] The wedding date was set for October 27, 1880, the prospective groom's twenty-second birthday.

∾

ON JUNE 30, Theodore graduated *magna cum laude* from Harvard with a class rank of 21 out of 177. But even without his academic achievements, it was one of the happiest times of his life. Not only was he engaged to be married to Alice, but his writing was showing great promise.

At the time of his graduation, Theodore had drafted the first two chapters of his book, *The Naval War of 1812*, an account of the war at sea that he hoped would be more thorough and objective than the standard British and American accounts. He had had an interest in naval affairs from the time he was a child, when his mother would share stories of the exploits of his uncle, James Dunwoody Bulloch, an officer in the Confederate navy during the Civil War. According to his later friend, Jacob Riis, Roosevelt also undertook the project in part to correct what he perceived to be errors in the account written by William James, which he had discovered in the Harvard library.

In *The Naval War of 1812* Roosevelt argued that presidents beginning with Thomas Jefferson largely scrapped the enhancement of American naval forces begun by George Washington and John Adams, thus allowing the British to start the War of 1812 against a United States navy that was weak and unprepared. But years later he acknowledged a few problems with his handling of the material: "Those chapters were so dry that they would have made a dictionary seem light reading by comparison."[6] Theodore eventually got some help and published the book in 1882 to critical acclaim. Its stress on the importance of a strong navy caused shockwaves that would reverberate down to his presidency and beyond.

The Harvard years had satisfied young Roosevelt. He said he had "a dozen good and true friends in college . . . [and] a lovely home; I have had but little work, only enough to give me an occupation, and to crown all—infinity above everything else put together—I have won the heart of the sweetest of girls for my wife. No man ever had so pleasant a college course."[7] His friend, William Roscoe Thayer, believed that "Harvard College was of inestimable value to Roosevelt because it enabled him to find himself—to be a man with his fellow men."[8]

One event that cast something of a shadow over Theodore's final days at Harvard was a physical exam. It revealed that he had an irregular heartbeat, the combined result of severe childhood asthma and his intense levels of physical activity. Theodore didn't tell anyone about the exam, including Alice. The college's physician, one Dr. Dudley A. Sargeant, recommended that the young man choose a sedentary occupation and even recommended that he stop running up and down the stairs if he wished to live a long life. Theodore was defiant. "Doctor," he exclaimed, "I'm going to do all the things you tell me not to do. If I've got to live the sort of life you have described, I don't care how short it is."[9]

In mid-August, two months before the wedding, Theodore and his brother, Elliott, went on a six-week hunting trip that took them through Illinois and Iowa, then up into the Red River country of Minnesota. Much of this area was wilderness in Theodore's time, but he saw the landscape changing. Later he said, "I wanted to see the rude, rough, formative life in the Far West before it vanished. I went there just in time."[10] The brothers hunted birds such as grouse, quail, doves, ducks, and hawks. During the trip, Theodore's asthma returned, he was bitten by a snake, both his guns broke, and he was thrown out of a wagon on his head. As the air turned decidedly cooler, he began to yearn for home.

Returning to New York, Theodore enrolled at Columbia University Law School. As early as the year before, he had begun to think of being something other than a professional scientist. In an August 1879 entry in his diary, he had written, "I have been thinking very seriously about what I will do after leaving college . . . I will probably either pursue a scientific course, or else study law, preparatory for going into public life."[11] But Alice wasn't happy with the notion of being a scientist's wife. Less than a month after his engagement, Roosevelt hinted to a friend that he had switched career plans because of Alice's objections: "I . . . have made everything subordinate to winning her; so you can perhaps understand a change in my ideas as regards science, etc."[12]

Theodore didn't seem to be very passionate about law, but he had excelled in the subject at Harvard and he had relatives in the legal profession who would be able to get him a job after he had passed the bar exam. Then there was the advice from Harvard professor J. Lawrence

Laughlin, who told Roosevelt that men like him were more needed in politics than science. But his mind was made up. "I shall study law next year," he wrote, "and must there do my best, and work hard for my little wife."[13] Political involvement of some sort was hardly ruled out, though. Shortly before his Harvard commencement, he declared, "I am going to try and better the cause of government in New York City; I don't know exactly how."[14] This may have been an offhand comment, but those few words would prove to be more prophetic than even Roosevelt could have imagined.

∼

THEODORE AND ALICE were married on October 27, a beautiful warm day, at the crowded Unitarian Church in Brookline, Massachusetts. Many of Theodore's friends and family members from New York were guests, including his childhood friend, Edith Carow. Elliott Roosevelt was the best man. "It was the dearest little wedding," a friend noted in her diary. "Alice looked lovely and Theodore so happy and [he] responded [to the vows] in the most determined and Theodorelike tones."[15] Afterwards, the guests returned to the Lee family home in Chestnut Hill to toast the newlyweds with champagne. Everybody had a good time. Edith Carow, for one, is said to have "danced the soles off her shoes."[16]

After the reception, the couple enjoyed a two-week honeymoon at Oyster Bay. "We breakfast at ten," Theodore wrote, "dine at two, and take tea at seven. . . . In the morning we got out driving in the buggy, behind [their horse] Lightfoot . . . In the afternoon we play tennis or walk in Fleets woods. In the evenings I read aloud . . ."[17] Now of legal voting age, Theodore slipped away on November 2 to vote in the presidential election for the successful Republican ticket of James A. Garfield and Chester A. Arthur. Looking back, he reminisced, "I doubt there was ever a happier honeymoon than ours has been."[18]

The young couple returned to the Roosevelt home on West Fifty-seventh Street in New York on November 13, welcomed by Theodore's mother and sisters. Theodore's first day at law school was only four days off, and they needed time to move into their new home.

As he settled into married life, Theodore had reached a turning point. Full of youthful exuberance, he was looking to make his mark on the world. All that was missing was something that would require his best efforts, something that would make Alice proud. With the $125,000 fortune he had inherited from his father, though, he had the luxury of waiting for opportunities to present themselves.

CHAPTER FIVE

Law, Then Politics

ONCE BACK in New York, Theodore did his best to fill his father's shoes. He was elected a trustee of several family charities, including the Orthopedic Dispensary and the New York Infant Asylum. And as his father had, he began taking his Sunday dinner with the orphans of the Newsboys' Lodging House. He also joined the National Prison Association and the Free Trade Club. Despite these efforts, Theodore saw that he didn't share his father's gifts. "I tried faithfully to do what Father had done but I did it poorly," he said years later. "In the end I found out that we each have to work in his own way to do our best; and when I struck mine, though it differed from his, yet I was able to follow the same lines and do what he would have had me do."[1]

Meanwhile, Roosevelt began his law studies. Most mornings, beginning at 7:30, he defied the advice of Harvard's Dr. Sargeant and walked the fifty-four blocks (or six miles) from his home, past the mansions of Fifth Avenue to Columbia University, which was then located on the city's Upper East Side. Even at Theodore's customarily brisk pace, the journey took a good forty-five minutes. He didn't want to arrive late because he enjoyed the morning lecture of Professor T.W. Dwight. There was also the problem of space in the lecture hall—those who arrived late were obliged either to squeeze next to the lectern or perch semi-precariously on the window sills.

Theodore loved to pepper his law professors with questions.

Professor Dwight, with his cold logic, seems to have been a favorite target. The bespectacled Roosevelt had a habit of leaping to his feet and arguing "for justice against legalism" and condemning the idea of *caveat emptor* (Latin for "Let the buyer beware"). He reflected later in his autobiography:

> The "let the buyer beware" maxim, when translated into actual practice, whether in law or business, tends to translate itself further into the seller making his profit at the expense of the buyer, instead of by a bargain which shall be to the profit of both.[2]

Even at such a young age, Theodore seems to have felt the need for society—or even government—to take an active role in preventing the powerful from taking advantage of the weak. He was no doubt aware of the various social reform movements that were gathering steam during that time. Those involved were appalled at the poor conditions under which many Americans, and particularly recent immigrants, lived. These advocates of the so-called "Social Gospel" believed that wide-ranging reforms were needed to address social and economic problems caused by rapid industrialization, urbanization, and an increasingly diverse population. Reformers such as Lyman Abbott and Washington Gladden pushed for the abolition of child labor, strong labor unions, factory safety, bans on alcohol, and improved public health measures. They lived in hope of a Golden Age: "If the twentieth century could do for us in the control of social forces what the nineteenth did for us in the control of natural forces, our grandchildren would be justified in regarding our present social life as semi-barbarous."[3]

Despite its attractions, Roosevelt wasn't entirely satisfied with law. Walking back and forth from school every day gave Theodore a chance to reflect on his studies and think about the legal profession. Many of his classmates aspired to become attorneys for large corporations, but Theodore didn't find the prospect very appealing. He believed that "big business" tended to use the law as a cover for predatory business practices. A classmate recalled that Theodore "never seemed to have the air of an attorney or of a professional student, but it was evident that he was one of the best men there, considered as a man."[4]

Over time, Theodore decided that his ideals of honesty and justice were a far cry from what he was learning at Columbia. He recalled that most of his work in law school involved defending property rights, with little attention paid to questions of ethics or morality. Theodore had clearly learned important lessons from his father about the awesome responsibility and obligation the rich and powerful had in serving society's less fortunate.

⌁

THEODORE AND ALICE had a lively social life in New York, and in short order they became part of the city's elite, hobnobbing with the likes of the fabulously wealthy Vanderbilts and Astors. They went to receptions, dinners, society balls, and theater parties. According to Theodore, their popularity in certain social circles was due in no small part to Alice. A member of Boston's ruling class, she amazed their friends in New York with her intelligence and grace. "Alice is universally and greatly admired," Theodore wrote, "and she seems to grow more beautiful day by day. How happy she has made me."[5]

Alice worked hard to become a part of her husband's world. She joined a sewing circle, had tea parties on Tuesday afternoons, and like Theodore became a member of Fifth Avenue Presbyterian Church. Most important, she was successful in winning the love of her husband's mother and sisters. Years later, Theodore's sister, Corinne, remembered that the family first thought Alice "was young and attractive," but later came to see that her "abilities lay below the surface."[6]

⌁

AT FIRST GLANCE, Theodore Roosevelt didn't seem like a man who would do well in the dog-eat-dog world of politics. He was wealthy, with an air of superiority, and he believed that politics was dirty business. Still, he wanted to make a difference in the lives of others, but he

Fifth Avenue on holiday. At the turn of the century, New York was a city of contrasts. Although Roosevelt lived in the wealthy "silk stocking" district, he was aware of the need for social reform early in his career. *National Archives*

knew he wasn't cut out for charity work. His passion for social justice was growing, and he needed an outlet for it. Someone had to oppose the sophistry of businessmen and lawyers.

In 1880, Theodore had registered as a Republican, his father's party and the party of Lincoln. Wealthy Americans typically supported Republican candidates because the "Grand Old Party" favored tariffs designed to protect American industries from foreign imports. More than any other issue, the tariff distinguished Republicans from Democrats, and the business community supported it. Republicans also linked protection of business interests with protection of all Americans held dear—family, community, and virtue. They attempted to paint the free-trade Democrats as anti-American and anti-capitalist. One Republican stalwart quipped, "The Democratic Party is a party of famine; it is a good friend of an early frost; it believes in the Colorado beetle and the weevil."[7]

Roosevelt wanted to do more than simply cast a vote. When he asked his wealthy friends about joining the local Republican Association, they tried to talk him out of it. As he wrote later, "these men—and the big business men and the lawyers also—laughed at me, and told me that politics were 'low'; that the organizations were not controlled by gentlemen; that I would find them run by saloon-keepers, horse-car conductors, and the like . . . that the men I met would be rough and brutal and unpleasant to deal with."[8]

Roosevelt wasn't discouraged. He went over and joined the Twenty-first District Republican Association in Morton Hall, which was actually a room over a saloon. The blue-collar Republican Party officials there were initially wary of him, but Theodore did all he could to earn their trust and friendship. They soon came to see that the charismatic young man with a well-known last name could do good things for the Republican cause in New York.

One of the officials Theodore met in Morton Hall was an Irishman named Joe Murray. He showed Theodore that those in politics didn't have to be greedy and dishonest. Theodore wrote that he was surprised that Murray was "by nature a straight man, as fearless and staunchly loyal as any one whom I have ever met, a man to be trusted in any position demanding courage, integrity, and good faith."[9] A major obstacle to Theodore running for office had been removed.

Encouraged by his first exposure to party politics, Roosevelt made a speech on behalf of a Republican measure in the State Assembly in Albany to reform New York's street-cleaning operations. The passionate speech was interrupted by applause several times. The measure didn't pass, but Theodore had shown himself and others that he could make a career out of politics. As a politician, he would no longer be Thee's son. He could chart his own course, the one best suited to his talents.

∾

IN THE SUMMER of 1881, after his first year at Columbia, Theodore and Alice went on a four-month honeymoon to Europe. It was his third trip to Europe, but his first as an adult. Theodore played the part of tour guide for his wife, and after Alice overcame her seasickness during the voyage across the Atlantic, the trip went well. They were enthralled by the green, pristine beauty of Ireland, enjoyed the botanical gardens of England, marveled at the paintings of Peter Paul Rubens at the Louvre in Paris, and shared their breakfast with pigeons in Venice.

In July, the honeymooners received the shocking news from home that President James Garfield—who had been in office for a few short months—had been shot in the spine by Charles Guiteau, a mentally unstable man. Garfield, head of the moderate Republican faction, clung to life for a few excruciatingly painful months, eventually succumbing to blood poisoning on September 19. "Frightful calamity for America," Theodore wrote in his diary. "This means work in the future for those who wish their country well."[10] Perhaps he was beginning to realize that he would be one of those doing the work.

But that would come later. For the moment, the young couple continued with their honeymoon, and in Switzerland, Theodore faced the high point of his trip—emotionally and physically—when he successfully climbed the Matterhorn. Nearly 15,000 feet high, the mountain was far easier to climb in the 1880s than in 1865, when the first assault was made, because of the installation of cables and the use of trained guides. Nonetheless, the climb was still taxing, especially for an amateur with a history of asthma, but he managed to reach the summit in two days.

This would be just one of many physically demanding challenges that Roosevelt would undertake. He had "made his body" as a boy, but as a man he would test himself relentlessly throughout his life.

∽

ONCE HOME, Theodore wasted no time in picking up where he had left off. A week after their ship docked in October, he was back at Columbia for his second year of law school. He also was putting the finishing touches on *The Naval War of 1812*, the book that would forever establish him as a military historian of the highest caliber. Theodore wrote a total of thirty-eight books in his lifetime, but this one was the most influential. When it was published in 1882, a copy was placed on all American naval vessels. Due in part to its influence, as well as to Roosevelt's leadership, the United States began to build its naval power at the end of the nineteenth century. And when Roosevelt became president, a strong navy was high on his agenda.

The year 1881 proved momentous because it saw the start of Theodore's political career. On October 28, he accepted the nomination as the Republican candidate for the New York State Assembly from the Twenty-first District. Because of the formal townhouses and the wealth of its residents, the district was called the "brownstone" or "silk stocking" district.

Theodore's family had had a long history of public service—his uncle, Robert Barnwell Roosevelt, was a United States congressman—and he had attended a half dozen Republican meetings at Morton Hall. When Joe Murray first asked Roosevelt to consider running for office, Theodore had said that he would only accept the nomination if Murray couldn't find another candidate. Unknown to Roosevelt, Murray had already decided on him. He had a famous last name as well as connections to wealthy voters who were growing weary of "politics as usual." When the Irishman claimed that he hadn't found another candidate, Roosevelt accepted the nomination.

Theodore threw himself completely into the campaign. He ran on a pledge to clean up New York City government, which had fallen into the corrupt hands of politicians beholden to wealthy elites. Roosevelt told the *New York Herald* on November 1 that, if elected, he would go to the state capital in Albany "untrammeled and unpledged" and that he "would obey no boss and serve no clique." The *New York Times* supported his candidacy, writing, "Every good citizen has cause for rejoicing that the Republicans of the twenty-first Assembly District have united upon so admirable a candidate for the Assembly as Mr. THEODORE ROOSEVELT."[11]

But Roosevelt was a novice in the area of practical politics, and it showed. His friend and biographer, William Roscoe Thayer, related one incident when candidate Roosevelt met some of the powerbrokers in his district—the influential saloonkeepers on Sixth Avenue:

> Accordingly, [Republican leaders] Jake Hess and Joe Murray proceeded to introduce Roosevelt to the rum-sellers of Sixth Avenue. The first [ones] they visited received Theodore with injudicious condescension almost as if he were a suppliant. [They] said [they] hoped that the young candidate, if elected, would treat the liquor men fairly, to which the "suppliant" replied that he intended to treat all interests fairly. The suggestion that liquor licenses were too high brought the retort that they were not high enough. Thereupon, the wary Hess and the discreet Joe Murray found an excuse for hurrying Roosevelt out of the saloon, and they told him that he had better look after his friends on Fifth Avenue and that they would look after the saloon-keepers on Sixth Avenue.[12]

Thanks to the unlikely alliance of the liquor interests on Sixth Avenue and the Fifth Avenue business and social leaders who had known and respected his father, Theodore decisively defeated his Democratic opponent. At twenty-three years old, he had won a seat on the New York State Assembly in Albany. His political star was only just beginning to rise.

Chapter Six

On to Albany

DURING HIS CAMPAIGN, Theodore's combination of reformist zeal and family background had made him the darling of New York's newspaper reporters. They followed him to Albany, confident that he would continue to make news. To reporters, he was different from the typical state politician. It remained to be seen, however, whether Roosevelt's passion for reform would cool once he took his seat in the Assembly. The question was on everyone's lips: Would Roosevelt follow the example of others and line his pockets with bribes from special interests?

Roosevelt thoroughly enjoyed himself in Albany. Years later in his autobiography, he wrote, "To a young man, life in the New York Legislature was always interesting and often entertaining. There was always a struggle of some kind on hand."[1] George Spinney of the *New York Times* described him as "a good hearted man to shake hands with and he had a good, honest laugh. You could hear him for miles, and it was not an affected laugh…teeth seemed to be all over his face. He was genial, emphatic, earnest but green as grass."[2] In addition, he had whiskers, and his glasses dangled on a silk cord that ran over his ear.

Roosevelt was the youngest member of the Assembly and one of sixty-one Republican members. There were sixty-seven Democrats, but eight of them were linked with Tammany Hall, New York City's corrupt Democratic organization, and the worst of corrupt state politics. "Tammany thus holds the balance of power," Theodore wrote,

"and as the split between her and the regular [Democrats] is very bit-
ter, a long deadlock is promised us."[3] He was proved correct, and the
Tammany Democrats were a thorn in his side for his entire time in
Albany.

From the outset, Theodore was not popular with his colleagues.
Both Democrats and Republicans thought he was an arrogant political
amateur. Democratic newspapers in New York referred to him as "his
Lordship" and "the exquisite Mr. Roosevelt." Roosevelt didn't have
many nice things to say about his colleagues, either. Many Republicans
were "bad enough," he wrote in his diary, but the Democrats were even
worse.[4]

In spite of this, there were lighter moments. He recalled that
"there were all kinds of humorous incidents, the humor being usually
of the unconscious kind." On one occasion, Roosevelt noted that a fellow assemblyman from New York City made a telling confession:

> On one occasion he had a bill to appropriate money, with obvious impro-
> priety, for the relief of some miscreant whom he styled "one of the hon-
> est yeomanry of the State." When I explained to him that it was clearly
> unconstitutional, he answered, "Me friend, the Constitution don't touch
> little things like that," and then added, with an ingratiating smile,
> "Anyhow, I'd never allow the Constitution to come between friends."[5]

In the State Assembly, Roosevelt was given a sought-after seat on
the Committee on Cities, where he could better look after the interests
of his constituents back home. But he wasn't pleased with his fellow
committee members. "Altogether the Committee is about as bad as it
could possibly be; most of the members are corrupt, and the others are
really singularly incompetent," he wrote.[6]

Theodore never doubted the moral rightness of his beliefs. Some
of his critics charged that he saw every issue as black and white, with
no room for finding a middle ground. A few even suspected that he was
conducting something resembling a religious crusade. Despite his
eccentricities, Roosevelt—or TR, as he was often called—quickly

developed a reputation for integrity, which was refreshing to many outside the world of politics. He recalled, "During my three years' service in the Legislature I worked on a very simple philosophy of government. It was that personal character and initiative are the prime requisites in political and social life . . . Fundamentally, our fight was part of the eternal war against the Powers that Prey; and we cared not a whit in what rank of life these powers were found."[7]

Early on, Roosevelt the reformer wanted to discover those men who were corrupt. He found to his anger and surprise that a full one-third of the politicians in Albany allegedly sold their votes to the highest bidder. A close friend said of TR that, "He objected earnestly to a man who was incompetent, but his whole nature revolted against one who had a bad character."[8] Because Theodore wouldn't sell his own vote, those who wanted certain bills passed in Albany asked for his support so that everyone would know the bills had merit.

～

ALTHOUGH ONLY ONE of his reform proposals was passed, Roosevelt had shown himself to be willing to take on the political establishment. After his first year in the State Assembly came to a close on June 2, 1882, he was praised by Republican newspapers and magazines as well as by reform groups. The year had been one of enormous intellectual growth for Theodore, and colleagues marveled how quickly he had surmounted a steep learning curve. As Charles Evans Hughes, then a law student and later a Supreme Court justice, recalled, "He was not [in the Assembly] for very long before everyone was impressed with his marked individuality. . . . It was a splendid breeze blowing through the legislative halls and making everyone feel brighter and better."[9]

The summer of 1882 was restful by Theodore's standards. On June 12, he joined the New York National Guard and was commissioned a second lieutenant. He also caught up on his law studies at Columbia and moved with Alice into their own home, a brownstone at 55 West Forty-fifth Street.

In the fall, Republicans nominated Theodore for a second year term in the State Assembly. In his major campaign address, he reaffirmed his opposition to large corporations that were motivated solely by economic self-interest. He saw them as a threat to basic human rights: "We as a people are suffering from new dangers," he said. "As our fathers fought with slavery and crushed it, in order that it would not seize and crush them, so we are called on to fight new forces."[10]

In the New York statewide elections of November 1882, the energetic and dashing forty-three-year-old Democrat Grover Cleveland was swept into the governor's office with a majority of 192,000 votes, bringing many other Democratic candidates with him. Roosevelt's popularity in his district was such, however, that he was reelected by some 2,000 votes. That was a greater majority than he had received in the previous year. A week after the election, though, Roosevelt lamented that "the next House will contain a rare set of scoundrels, and we Republicans will be in such a hopeless minority that I do not see clearly what we can accomplish, even in checking bad legislation."[11]

Theodore was chosen by the shell-shocked Republicans, now clearly in the minority, to be their leader, and he also headed up a reformist group of lawmakers known as "Roosevelt Republicans." Alice, who had accompanied Theodore to Albany during his first term in office, now lived in their Manhattan townhouse while Theodore stayed in Albany during the week and commuted to New York on the weekends.

The balance of power was now squarely in favor of the Democrats and Governor Cleveland, so Theodore and the Republicans were forced to join with them to pass important legislation. Working with the governor, Theodore crafted a civil service reform bill that Cleveland signed into law. The purpose of the bill was to attempt to remove (or at least reduce) the influence of money on the administration of state government.

Despite his call for government to be honest and fair to all people, as a wealthy man Theodore had an imperfect understanding of how ordinary men and women lived. Their situation was increasingly dire in the wake of the economic depression that began in 1882 and lasted for several years. In New York City, the depression meant that nearly half the work force was unemployed, and wages for those who managed to find work were reduced to as little as $2 a day. Even more appalling was the fact that many worked twelve- or sixteen-hour days, in the face of stiff competition from new immigrants, to earn such wages. All the while the rich spent thousands on elaborate balls, ornate floral decorations, and all manner of food and wine.

At this early point in his political career, Roosevelt supported low wages, low taxes, and limited government. He voted against cutting the working hours of streetcar conductors from fifteen to twelve, and he also opposed a proposal by hatmakers that would have stopped prisoners from making hats at a lower cost. Roosevelt believed that, if left alone by the government, most people would (and could) strive to better themselves and climb the economic ladder.

It would be a mistake, however, to assume that Roosevelt was instinctively anti-labor. In a speech on the floor of the State Assembly, he protested, "I represent neither capital nor labor. I represent every American citizen, be he a laborer or be he capitalist . . . I can only say that I will try to do them justice as I have tried to do all other classes justice."[12]

During his second year in the State Assembly, Samuel Gompers, a prominent labor leader and head of the Cigarmakers' Union, appealed to Roosevelt's sense of justice. He took Theodore on a tour of tenement apartments where Bohemian immigrants who didn't speak English— whole families—worked sixteen to eighteen-hour days rolling cigars by hand. All told, they made over a third of the 670 million cigars that were produced each year in New York City. As a result of the horrific conditions he witnessed, Theodore supported a bill then before the Assembly banning the manufacture of cigars in such buildings. He wrote, "Whatever the theories might be, as a matter of practical common sense I could not conscientiously vote for the continuance of the conditions which I saw."[13]

The bill passed and was signed by Governor Cleveland in 1883, but it was then declared unconstitutional by the courts. Roosevelt got a modified version of the bill passed in 1884, but once again the courts overturned it. Irate, Roosevelt began to think that some court decisions "were erected as bars across the path of social reform, and . . . brought to naught so much of the effort to secure justice and fair dealing for workingmen and workingwomen, and for plain citizens generally."[14]

Throughout his later years in Albany, Roosevelt was a strong supporter of legislation to improve working conditions and require safety measures in factories. Thinking they were politically motivated, though, he voted against pay increases for policemen, firemen, and city workers. In 1883, he did support a bill to roll back the fare on Manhattan Elevated Railway from ten to five cents. The sponsors of the bill were disingenuous, however, because they did not really favor a fare rollback. Rather, they hoped for kickbacks from the railway, and then they would withdraw the bill. No money was forthcoming, but by then the bill had garnered widespread popular support and withdrawing it at that point would have been politically dangerous. The bill went on to pass both houses of the legislature—the Assembly and the Senate—but Governor Cleveland vetoed it, citing the state's previous agreement to provide the railway with a certain level of operational income.

Like many other legislators, Roosevelt had supported the bill. But in light of Cleveland's veto, and as the legislature sought an override, Roosevelt had a change of heart. He took to the floor of the Assembly and gave his reasons:

> I have to confess that I weakly yielded, partly in a vindictive spirit towards the infernal thieves and conscienceless swindlers who have had the elevated railroad in charge and partly to the popular voice of New York. For the managers of the elevated railroad I have as little feeling as any man here . . . I regard these men as furnishing part of that most dangerous of all dangerous classes, the wealthy criminal class. Nevertheless,

it is not a question of doing justice to them, it is a question of doing justice to ourselves. . . . [15]

Like Cleveland, Roosevelt believed in being fair. The state had made a promise, and it must honor that promise. In the end, Cleveland's veto stood, and TR's conscience was clear once again. It would not be the last time, however, that he would face the combined forces of wealth and power. Indeed as president, they were always in his sights.

CHAPTER SEVEN

"The Light Has Gone Out of My Life"

IN THE SUMMER of 1883, as New Yorkers marveled at the newly opened Brooklyn Bridge, the "Eighth Wonder of the World," Theodore's attention turned to his personal life. After nearly two years of marriage, Alice was pregnant. Theodore the politician was about to become Theodore the father.

On their honeymoon, Theodore had shown Alice around his family's home in Oyster Bay on Long Island, New York. He said he would build a home for them on the summit of Sagamore Hill, the same place where he used to recite poetry as a boy. With Alice expecting their first child, Theodore made good on his promise. He had already spent $30,000 to purchase 155 acres of land on Long Island, and after selling some of it to relatives, he had architects begin work on a sprawling home on the remaining ninety-five acres. The house was to include a wraparound porch where he and Alice could sit in rocking chairs and admire the sunset, as well as twelve bedrooms, quarters for the servants, a large library, and several fireplaces. There would also be an abundance of stained glass. When finished, it would be a mansion of twenty-two rooms (another was added later). In honor of Alice, the house would be called Leeholm.

In September, with Alice four months pregnant, Theodore left to go buffalo hunting on the Little Missouri River just east of the Montana line, in the Badlands of the Dakota Territory. Commander H.

Huge, rambling, and comfortable, Sagamore Hill would be Theodore's beloved summer home for his entire life. *Library of Congress*

H. Gorringe, the owner of a hunting ranch there, had invited him, and Theodore jumped at the chance, but when Gorringe backed out at the last minute, he went alone rather than lose the money he had invested in the trip. When he went, Alice's eyes were puffy and her ankles were swollen, and Roosevelt's mother noted how "very large" she looked. Perhaps feeling guilty at leaving his wife in such a state, Theodore promised to bring Alice home a buffalo's head and the antlers of two large deer. One can imagine how Alice received the gifts. If Theodore had had any idea of how seriously ill his wife really was, there seems little doubt that he would have stayed home.

Arriving via the new Northern Pacific Railroad, Theodore set foot for the first time in the Badlands, an untamed corner of North America that promised a life in every respect different from the pampered existence he had known in New York. The wide open spaces and the natural beauty of the western land enchanted him. He wrote to Alice that he hadn't taken off his dirty clothes in two weeks, and added, "but I sleep, eat and work as I never could do in ten years in the city."[1]

Roosevelt always felt the most free and at peace when he was tramping through the woods, climbing a mountain, or sloshing through a foamy stream. From the time his father had told him he must "make" his body, Theodore believed that manliness was bound up with adventure and athleticism. A man proved his worth, even his patriotism, by challenging the elements—animal, vegetable, and mineral—and triumphing over them. There was something very visceral, something pulse-quickening, in this Rooseveltian approach to life. Many years later in *A Book-Lover's Holidays in the Open*, he wrote of the freedom a person feels when

> he can see the red splendor of desert sunsets, and the unearthly glory of the afterglow on the battlements of desolate mountains. In sapphire gulfs of ocean he can visit islets, above which the wings of myriads of sea-fowl make a kind of shifting cuneiform script in the air. He can ride along the brink of the stupendous cliff-walled canyon, where eagles soar below him, and cougars make their lairs on the ledges and harry the big-horned sheep. He can journey through the northern forests, the home of the giant moose, the forests of fragrant and murmuring life in summer, the iron-bound and melancholy forests of winter.[2]

The Badlands at that time were populated by dangerous animals, as well as by restive Sioux Indians, the same tribe that had killed Lt.-Col. George Armstrong Custer and 264 of his men at the battle of the Little Bighorn in 1876. "It was still the Wild West in those days," Roosevelt recalled, "the Far West, the West of Owen Wister's stories and Frederic Remington's drawings, the West of the Indian and the buffalo-hunter, the soldier and the cow-puncher."[3]

Roosevelt loved almost every minute of his time in the Badlands. After his train deposited him and pulled away, Roosevelt carried his guns and his duffel bag to the nearby Pyramid Park Hotel in Little Missouri, Dakota

Territory. Within days, he and Canadian Joe Ferris were hunting buffalo, although the numbers of the great beast had dwindled dramatically due to overhunting. Soon, however, Roosevelt's thoughts turned to cattle. He had seen many ranches on the trip. Convinced that a ranch could prosper by supplying beef via railway to dinner tables in the eastern United States, Roosevelt invested $14,000 in 400 head of cattle, which he left in the care of two new business partners. He bought an interest in two cattle ranches—the Chimney Butte and the Elkhorn—as well.

Upon his return, Roosevelt was reelected to a third term in the New York State Assembly in November 1883. The political balance of power had shifted again, and Republicans now had the majority of seats in Albany. Roosevelt was named chairman of the powerful Committee on Cities. That fall he introduced bills to increase the power of mayors and convinced his colleagues to appoint a five-man investigating committee, with himself as the chairman, to probe corruption in the government of New York City. He also sponsored a bill to reduce corruption in the New York City sheriff's office.

Knowing that Alice would be lonely at home while he was in Albany, he arranged for her to stay with his sister, Conie. Conie was a new mother herself, and the two women planned to start a nursery on the third floor of her house on West Fifty-seventh Street. Theodore's mother and other sister, Bamie, were also both there.

∾

ON FEBRUARY 12, 1884, while Theodore was in legislative session in Albany, Alice went into labor and delivered an 8 ¾-pound baby girl. An exhausted Alice said, "I love a little girl," briefly held the child in her arms, and then fell asleep. A telegram reached Theodore with the news that the baby was healthy, but that Alice was "only fairly well." Not thinking much of the news about Alice's condition, Theodore accepted the congratulations from his fellow lawmakers and prepared to take a joyous train ride home to New York later in the day.

Within a few hours, a second telegram arrived. Theodore was to get to New York immediately. He rushed home and made it there by midnight. As he approached the house, he was greeted by his brother, Elliott, who said, "There is a curse on this house. Mother is dying and Alice is dying, too."[4]

Barely able to believe what he was hearing, Theodore raced up the stairs, two at a time, to Alice's bedroom. By the time he arrived, she was barely conscious and hardly recognized him. The doctor who was attending to the women said that Alice had Bright's disease, an inflammation of the kidneys. Although treatable today, at the time it was presumed fatal. Unable to do anything for his wife, Theodore held Alice in his arms for two hours as she clung to life. Alice died the next day, on February 14, the fourth anniversary of their engagement. She was only twenty-two years old.

Cut down, too, was Theodore's mother, Martha, who had died of typhoid the night before at the age of forty-nine. As he watched her die, in the same house where his father had died six years earlier, Theodore exclaimed, "There *is* a curse on this house."[5] When Alice died a few hours later, the curse was complete.

During his engagement to Alice, Theodore had said, "life will always seem laughing and loving." On the night of February 14, 1884, Theodore drew a large cross in his diary and wrote underneath it, "The light has gone out of my life."[6]

Less than forty-eight hours later, there was a double funeral at Fifth Avenue Presbyterian Church. Over two thousand mourners attended, including members of the wealthy Astor banking family and the Vanderbilts of railroad fame. Theodore was absolutely distraught. According to a friend who saw him at the funeral, Theodore was "in a dazed, stunned state. He does not know what he says or does."[7] In the days after Alice's death, family members could hear the sound of him pacing in his room, all alone.

The day after the funeral of her mother and grandmother, Theodore's infant daughter was christened Alice Lee. At her christening, she wore a locket containing a lock of her mother's hair.

Unable to care for his daughter and continue with his duties in the State Assembly, Theodore left Alice with his sister, Bamie, at her home on 422 Madison Avenue in New York. Bamie, who was twenty-nine years old and without any viable marriage prospects, was happy to care for Baby Lee. Later in life Alice Lee would say that Bamie was "the only one I really cared about when I was a child. . . . She was the single most important influence on my childhood."[8]

Within a week of his wife's death, Theodore returned to Albany, where his colleagues stood in silent tribute as he took his seat. Presently he threw himself into his work, confiding to one friend that work was the only thing protecting his sanity.

Theodore's grief over the death of his beloved Alice was so intense that he never wanted to talk about her. He didn't mention her name in his autobiography or talk about her to anyone, including their daughter, and he burned some of the reminders of their life together. In the end, as Theodore sectioned off the damaged corners of his heart, it was almost as if Alice had never existed.

His daughter, Alice, hinted years later that she had wished that her father had been more open about her mother's death. "The whole thing was really handled very badly," she recalled. "It was awfully bad psychologically."[9] In later years, Alice Lee Roosevelt's emotional wounds would harden first into a callus of detachment and ultimately into exaggerated teenage rebellion.

The final words Theodore wrote about his wife Alice sum up their life together: "Fair, pure, and joyous as a maiden; loving, tender, and happy as a young wife . . . when my heart's dearest died, the light went from my life for ever."[10]

◦

IN THE WAKE of Alice's death, Theodore showed a new willingness to work with other members of the State Assembly in getting legislation passed. There was more to life, he now realized, than winning an argument. He had come to see that politics was the art of compromise. As a result, many of his reform measures were passed. On one day in April 1884, the Assembly passed seven bills.

Roosevelt had another lesson in "real" politics later that year. Although he had declined to run for a fourth term as assemblyman, in the summer of 1884 he and three other Mugwumps ("Independent or Anti-Machine Republicans"[11] not tied to corruption within the party), were selected as New York delegates to the Republican National Convention in Chicago. Here Roosevelt worked to get a reformist, Senator George Edmunds of Vermont, nominated. The Republican Party establishment, however, nominated James G. Blaine instead.

TR considered Blaine to be one of the most corrupt politicians in America. When he was selected as the Republican candidate, an Ohio congressman named William McKinley urged Theodore to make a speech at the convention in support of Blaine, but Roosevelt refused. After the convention, some Republicans who were also unhappy with Blaine's nomination left the party and openly supported Grover Cleveland, the Democratic candidate.

After much soul-searching, however, Roosevelt backed Blaine and worked for his unsuccessful presidential campaign. Roosevelt told reporters in October 1884 that it was "altogether contrary to my character to occupy a neutral position in so important and exciting a struggle . . . I made up my mind that it was clearly my duty to support the [Republican] ticket."[12]

The reformers who had placed their trust in Roosevelt's good sense during his years in the State Assembly were shocked that he had gone over to the Blaine camp. Some called him a "turncoat"; others said he wanted Blaine's support for a run for mayor of New York City. Alice's friends said TR's friend, Henry Cabot Lodge, an aristocratic Bostonian who was running for Congress in Massachusetts, had duped him.

Whatever the speculation, Theodore knew that he needed to support Blaine, and not Cleveland, if he was to have any future in the Republican Party. For almost the first time in his political career he had chosen pragmatism over principle, and surely it was not a comfortable choice. In his autobiography, written years later, Roosevelt sought to justify his decision by writing, "[Blaine's] nomination was won in fair and aboveboard fashion, because the rank and file of the party stood back of him; and I supported him to the best of my ability in the ensuing campaign."[13]

The issue of the protective tariff, which had helped the Republicans in 1880, did not play as central a role in the campaign of 1884. Instead the campaign was filled with personal attacks and weighed down by the revelation that Cleveland had fathered a child out of wedlock. On election eve, the historian Henry Adams commented, "We are here plunged in politics funnier than words can express. Very great issues are involved. . . . But the amusing thing is that no one talks about real interests. By common consent they agree to let these alone. We are afraid to discuss them."[14]

Blaine lost the election to Cleveland in an extremely close race. With his party out of the White House, and his principles compromised, Roosevelt was at a low point. He wrote to Cabot Lodge that he feared his political career was over. Having lost the support of his reformist friends in New York, and still coping with life as a widower, Theodore decided he needed to leave the political arena and get some fresh air on the western frontier. He returned to the Badlands, his refuge in times of trouble.

CHAPTER EIGHT

A Breath of Fresh Air

THEODORE HEADED to his ranch in the Badlands to regroup. Arriving in full cowboy gear, he stayed there for three years, although he did take frequent trips back to New York. A local western newspaper reported that Roosevelt was relishing life in the Badlands and hadn't given much consideration to a political comeback. Instead, Theodore was writing about the freedom he experienced, the excellent hunting opportunities, and the beautiful scenery. His experiences in the Dakota Territory formed the basis for three books: *Hunting Trips of a Ranchman* contained an account of a grizzly bear hunt, *Ranch Life and the Hunting Trail* discussed bighorn sheep, and *The Wilderness Hunter* explored the private life of the grizzly bear.

When he went out West, Theodore was still thin and frail-looking, but he soon developed into a strong man with a thick neck, muscular shoulders, and a powerful chest. He spoke of his improved health and of the long hours he spent riding on horseback.

Friend and biographer William Roscoe Thayer summarized Theodore's life as a rancher:

> At one time or another he performed all the duties of a ranchman. He went on long rides after the cattle, he rounded them up, he helped to brand them and to cut out the beeves destined for the Eastern market. He followed the herd when it stampeded during a terrific thunderstorm. In winter there was often need to save the wandering cattle from a sud-

den and deadly blizzard. The log cabin or "shack" in which he dwelt was rough, and so was the fare; comforts were few. He chopped the cotton-wood which they used for fuel; he knew how to care for the ponies; and once at least he passed more than twenty-four hours in the saddle with-out sleep. According to the best standards, he says, he was not a fine horseman, but it is clear that he could do everything with a horse which had to be done, and that he never stopped from fatigue. When they needed fresh meat, he would shoot it. In short, he held his own under all the hardships and requirements demanded of a cowboy or ranchman.[1]

The public back in New York who heard reports of Roosevelt's exploits saw him as a rough-riding cowboy rather than a city slicker from a famous family. Theodore was in no hurry to correct that impression, but in truth he was really a rancher who employed cowboys and only worked alongside them. His privileged background was not forgotten: his hunting knife came from Tiffany's and he had a fancy Winchester rifle. He also insisted on employees calling him "Mr. Roosevelt."

Theodore undoubtedly displayed considerable bravery while out in the Badlands. Once he knocked senseless a man who was threatening him with two revolvers in a hotel barroom. He served as a deputy sher-iff, and along with two others captured three men who had stolen a boat: "When they were within twenty yards or so we straightened up from behind the bank, covering them with our cocked rifles, while I shouted for them to hold up their hands," Roosevelt wrote.[2]

In 1885, a dispute arose between Theodore and the Marquis de Mores, a French-born entrepreneur who founded a settlement in the Badlands and was out to make his fortune in cattle. De Mores thought that a friend of Theodore's had gotten him into trouble with the law, and he wrote an angry letter to Roosevelt. Theodore understood this as a challenge to duel, and he reluctantly agreed. Thayer recalled, "Roosevelt despised dueling as a silly practice, which would not settle justice between disputants; but . . . any man who declined a challenge lost caste and had better leave the country at once."[3] A duel was averted

Theodore struck a determined studio pose, armed and in buckskin, before heading to the Badlands, 1885. *Photograph by George Grantham Bain. Library of Congress*

only after de Mores demurred. Theodore was fortunate: the marquis was a former army officer who had killed two other men in duels.

∼

THEODORE'S POLITICAL yearnings were dormant, but they never disappeared entirely. In September 1885, he arrived back in New York to attend the State Republican Convention at Saratoga. There the party selected its nominee for governor, Cornelius N. Bliss.

Over the next few months, while Theodore canvassed the state campaigning for Republican candidates, he caused some controversy when he wrote in the October issue of the *North American Review* that James G. Blaine, the 1884 Republican candidate, would have won the presidential election if blacks in the South had been allowed to vote. The passage of the Fourteenth Amendment to the Constitution at the end of the Civil War had declared blacks to be full citizens and therefore eligible to vote. In fact, Article II of the amendment laid out specific punishments for states that denied "the right to vote . . . [to] any of the male inhabitants of such State, being twenty-one years of age, and citizens of the United States." But the provision would not be enforced for another century. Southern states added requirements for voting such as literacy tests and ownership of property that effectively disenfranchised many black voters (and most poor whites as well). In the postwar South, blacks who objected to these restrictions faced reprisals from angry whites.

In his article, Roosevelt argued that blacks in the South should have been allowed to vote without restrictions because they were American citizens. Their vote may have changed the outcome of the election, which had been decided by only 30,000 votes out of over ten million cast. Roosevelt knew that many blacks would have voted for Blaine because the Republicans were still seen as the party of Abraham Lincoln, the man who signed the Emancipation Proclamation and freed the slaves. So strong was the perceived link between the Republican Party and the abolition of slavery that when Grover

Cleveland was the first Democrat elected president since the Civil War, many Southern blacks feared that slavery would be restored.[4]

~

WHILE THEODORE was taking stock of his life, friends and colleagues reported that he never talked about Alice Lee or his daughter. Once when he complained that he had nothing to live for, his friend Bill Sewall said, "You have your daughter to live for." Theodore responded, "Her aunt can take care of her a good deal better than I can."[5]

Losing his first love, his wife, was still far too painful. His blonde, blue-eyed daughter, the spitting image of her mother, may have brought to the surface too many emotions to bear. Consequently Baby Alice saw very little of her father during the first years of her life. He spent most of his time in the Badlands, trying to reconnect with the manly pursuits he had cast aside in order to pursue her mother.

In the fall of 1885, however, a chain of events was set in motion, one that soon brought Theodore and his daughter together. In October, a year and a half after the death of Alice Lee, Theodore came in from the Badlands and paid a visit to Bamie's home in New York City to see his daughter. He had given his sisters clear instructions to keep his childhood friend, Edith Carow, away when he came to visit. She lived only six blocks from Bamie on Twentieth Street. Edith had spent a lot of time at Bamie's home, and she was best friends with Theodore's other sister, Conie. Nevertheless, Theodore had successfully avoided her.

As he opened the front door this time, Edith was coming down the stairs and the two nearly collided. Edith was now twenty-four and more attractive than Theodore had remembered; her small hands and small feet gave her a graceful air. Almost despite himself, Theodore immediately rekindled a relationship with Edith that had been snuffed out years earlier when Alice Lee came upon the scene.

Theodore and Edith had known each other for their entire lives. Theodore, three years older, remembered seeing her in her crib as an infant. He was aware that Edith could be temperamental—he wrote to his sisters that she had her "good days" and her "bad days"—and was more comfortable with books than she was in social situations. Edith understood that Theodore was a dynamic human being, a force that could be moderated but never wholly tamed. Years later, Edith wrote, "One should not live to oneself. It was a temptation to me, only [Theodore] would not allow it."[6] For his part, Theodore knew that Edith's moderating influence was something he sorely needed:

> Greatly though I loved [Edith], I was at times thoughtless and selfish, and if [she] had been a more unhealthy Patient Griselda I might have grown in selfish and inconsiderate ways. [Edith], always tender, gentle and considerate, and always loving, yet, when necessary, pointed out where I was thoughtless, instead of submitting to it. Had she not done this, it would have made her life very much harder, and mine very much less happy.[7]

Some have suggested that Bamie was playing matchmaker, but whatever the case, Theodore and Edith quickly fell deeply in love. Prior to Alice Lee, they had discussed marriage, and nothing had come of it. But on November 17, 1885, only a month after their chance reunion, the pair became secretly engaged. There would be no more broken promises nor missed opportunities.

For whatever reason, Theodore and Edith resumed their individual routines after the engagement—Edith headed to Europe and Theodore returned to his Dakota ranch—and kept the news to themselves. Not even Theodore's sisters were privy to the fact that they would soon have a new sister-in-law. In August 1886, while Theodore was in the Badlands, the society page of the *New York Times* announced the engagement, but a week later Bamie placed a retraction, calling the report "erroneous" and "reprehensible."[8]

The next month, however, Theodore wrote a letter to Bamie, who was still caring for his daughter, and revealed that reports of his engagement were indeed true. But what is most interesting about the letter is that Theodore offered Bamie permanent custody of Alice. "As I have already told you," he wrote, "if you wish to you shall keep Baby Lee, I of course paying the expenses."[9] With an annual income of $2,600 from Bamie's substantial real estate holdings, the two would have enjoyed a comfortable future together.

It was not to be. By Christmas of 1886, as Theodore's marriage drew closer, he wrote to Bamie with some heartbreaking news. "I hardly know what to say about Baby Lee," he wrote. "Edith feels more strongly about her than I could have imagined possible. However, we can decide it all when we meet."[10]

Years later Bamie recalled, "It almost broke my heart to give her up."[11] By the time Alice was three, she had developed a devotion to Bamie that would remain throughout her life. Years later, when tensions with her father and stepmother developed, Bamie told Alice, "Remember, darling, if you are very unhappy you can always come back to me."[12] When Alice was a difficult fourteen-year-old, Theodore and Edith did dispatch her to Bamie's house for the summer, a move that was apparently much more agreeable to her parents than to Alice. "I have just received a letter from Alice," Edith wrote wryly to her sister, "saying it was 'worse than boarding-school,' little-knowing, poor child, that that was why I sent her."[13]

～

BEFORE THEODORE and Edith could think seriously about getting married, there was the small matter of Theodore's ranching operations. The problem was that Edith had no intention of being a rancher's wife in the Badlands. She was a very private person, only sporadically social, and she scorned those whom she felt to be intellectual lightweights. Surely she felt the cowboys of the untamed frontier fit into that latter category.

Fortunately for Theodore, the problem soon solved itself. Never very good at handling money, he had spent a great deal of his inheritance on cattle, a new ranch house, feed, and supplies in the Badlands. Despite his best efforts, the ranch had yet to turn a profit by 1886 due to a combination of low beef prices, a scorching drought across the northern plains, and the loss of ranch hands. Soon it was clear that Theodore's sizable investment would come to nothing. And any doubts were removed once and for all during the winter of 1886–87, which was the harshest anyone could remember. Storms decimated the animals that had been fortunate enough to survive the drought of the previous summer.

Theodore eventually realized that his days as a rancher would have to come to an end, and his thoughts returned to politics, a topic that was never far from his mind. The day before he left the daily running of his ranch to his assistants and returned home to New York in September 1886, he had a long talk with a friend in the Badlands. Still unsure about his future, and reeling from the loss of his investment in ranching, Theodore asked whether he should enter politics or law. The friend told him to enter politics "because such men as he didn't go into politics and they were needed in politics. If you go into politics and live, your chance to be President is good." Roosevelt laughed and said, "You have a good deal more faith in me than I have in myself. That looks a long ways ahead to me."[14]

Through his experiences in the Badlands, away from the comforts of home and the company of friends and family, Theodore showed himself to be a young man of undeniable grit. His resolve was tested more than once, and he emerged from the ordeals stronger than before. The lessons he learned out West would stay with him for the rest of his life. In the words of one historian, "He seems to have seen himself, not quite consciously, as like John the Baptist in the desert, or Jesus Christ spending a time in the wilderness to prepare himself for his ministry."[15]

≈

AFTER THEODORE arrived back in New York in the fall of 1886, a group of influential Republicans (and very possibly Edith) urged him to run for mayor of the city. He didn't think he had much chance of winning what ended up as a three-way race, but he wanted to get back into politics, so he accepted their offer. He became known as the "Cowboy Candidate" and campaigned vigorously, sometimes putting in eighteen-hour days and appearing at four or five campaign rallies a night. As he expected, however, he lost the election.

Regardless, he was in that joyous mood experienced only by those in love. Four days after the election, in the early hours of Saturday, November 6, Theodore and his sister Bamie set sail for England under the assumed names "Mr. and Mrs. Merrifield." The press was completely fooled, and the young people slipped away from shore undetected. On board Theodore met a British diplomat named Cecil Arthur Spring-Rice, and by the time they docked in England on November 13, he had agreed to be Theodore's best man at his wedding. In England Theodore, Bamie, and "Springy" (as Spring-Rice was nicknamed) met up with Edith Carow, who already was in London visiting her mother and her sister.

Theodore and Edith were married in St. George's Church, Hanover Square, in London on the morning of December 2. The day was especially foggy, even for London, and even the church was full of fog. Thanks to the bright orange gloves lent him by Spring-Rice, Edith could just barely make out Theodore as she walked down the aisle toward him, arm-and-arm with her brother, who gave away the bride.

Theodore's second turn at the altar was decidedly low-key. The church was nearly empty, and his mood had been dampened somewhat by his failed bid for mayor and the uncertain prospects for his ranch in the Badlands. A four-month honeymoon to France and Italy followed, and when the Roosevelts returned to New York in March 1887, they settled in Long Island at Sagamore Hill, which had formerly been known as Leeholm. The mansion had been finished in 1884, just months after Alice's death. Edith was already pregnant with their first child and anxious to settle down. The couple also officially took custody of three-year-old Baby Lee. During that year, Theodore got to know his daughter and found her "too good and cunning for anything."[16] Little Alice liked to watch her father shave and play tennis, and she wanted

Edith Carow, his childhood friend, won Theodore's heart—
even though he had tried to avoid her after Alice Lee's death.
Theodore Roosevelt Collection, Harvard College Library

him to carry her downstairs on piggyback to breakfast every morning.
On rainy days, Theodore and his young daughter would sit on the floor
and build forts with blocks.

Money was a worry, and Theodore cast about for new ways to earn
extra income. His ranching operation had folded, and it seemed that
the only family member with any money was his young daughter, Alice.
Her maternal grandparents, the Lees of Chestnut Hill, sent her regular cash payments, and she was receiving $2,000 a year by the age of
seventeen. She also had tens of thousands of dollars in annual income
from trust funds established by her grandparents. Perhaps only half-

joking, Theodore once quipped to Edith, "Be nice to Alice. We might have to borrow money from her one day."[17]

In his quest to fatten the family coffers, Roosevelt returned to writing, which in his adult years became a passion of his that was second only to politics. Through the influence of his powerful Republican friend, Senator Henry Cabot Lodge, Theodore was awarded a book contract by the Boston publishing house Houghton Mifflin. His first work was a biography of Missouri senator and western expansionist, Thomas Hart Benton. After the book received generally solid reviews from critics, Theodore set to work on a biography of the relatively unknown Founding Father, Gouvernor Morris. Researched and written in three months, the book was published in 1888 to mediocre reviews.

By this time, Theodore was producing a steady stream of magazine articles to help support his family, and he began work on a history of American westward expansion. *The Winning of the West*, a work in three volumes, was finished in 1895. It covered the years from 1774, when Daniel Boone crossed the Allegheny Mountains, to 1836, the year Davy Crockett died at the Alamo. By the time the third volume was finished, the "Wild West" had passed from reality into the realm of folklore and "Buffalo Bill" Cody's Wild West Show.

$\sim$

EVEN AS THEODORE's literary output was growing larger, so was the size of his family. His first child with Edith was born early in the morning of September 13, 1887. The first of four Roosevelt boys, he was christened Theodore Roosevelt Jr., but came to be known to the family simply as Ted. The evening of his birth Theodore added "Sr." to his own signature for the first time.

Little brother Ted fascinated Alice, now a big sister. She watched him from the vantage point of her small rocking chair, which she pulled close to Ted's crib. Unlike the events surrounding Alice's birth, this time the occasion was one of unmitigated joy and celebration. Theodore could not have been more pleased.

In short order, Edith gave birth to three more sons and a daughter—Kermit, born in 1889; Ethel, born in 1891; Archibald, born in 1894; and Quentin, born in 1897. Kermit, two years younger than Ted, was a dreamer with a vivid imagination and quick mind. Ethel, two years younger than Kermit, was temperamental and strong-willed. Unlike the older children, Archibald, or Archie as he came to be called, was born in Washington, D.C. Quentin, the youngest, was a lovable child who was born while Theodore was assistant secretary of the navy. He was the most outgoing of the Roosevelt children, making friends wherever he went.

Both Theodore and Edith loved their children, but they had a special place in Theodore's heart. In 1903, he wrote, "I love all these children and have great fun with them, and I am touched by the way in which they feel I am their special friend, champion, and companion."[18]

In turn, he was the center of his children's world. He marked their toy horses and cattle with brands of his western ranch and told them stories of his boyhood heroes. On rainy days, they played hide-and-seek. He taught his children the value of honesty and hard work. When the weather was good, and while Edith was working in her beloved flower garden, Theodore took his children, their cousins, and family friends on "scrambles" that were like obstacle courses. In this, Theodore harkened back to the endurance tests of his childhood:

> At Oyster Bay Roosevelt has instituted "hiking." He and the young people and such of the neighbors as chose would start from Sagamore Hill and walk in a bee-line to a point four or five miles off. The rule was that no natural impediment should cause them to digress or to stop. So they went through the fields and over the fences, across ditches and pools, and even clambered up and down a haystack, if one happened to be in the way, or through a barnyard.[19]

There's a delightful story Theodore told about how he tried to teach Kermit to read using a favorite book from his own childhood, a natural history by J.G. Wood titled *Homes Without Hands*. Because the letter

"H" was used in the title, he thought he could make "H" the first letter his son learned. "Whether it was the theory or my method of applying it that was defective I do not know," Roosevelt wrote later, "but I certainly absolutely eradicated from his brain any ability to learn what 'H' was; and long after he had learned all the other letters of the alphabet in the old-fashioned way, he proved wholly unable to remember 'H' under any circumstances."[20]

To the amazement and delight of his children, Theodore could—and did—speak about almost any subject. His son, Ted, recalled:

> His knowledge stretched from babies to the post-Alexandrian kingdoms and, what was more, he could always lay his hands on it. It made little difference in what channels the conversation turned. Sooner or later Father was able to produce information which often startled students of the theme under discussion.[21]

While Theodore's younger children enjoyed their active family life, Alice—who was called "Sister" within the family to avoid reference to her mother Alice Lee—did not. She referred to her father's family outings as "perfectly awful endurance tests masquerading as games!"[22] Unlike her siblings, Alice was not naturally athletic, but her father continued to push her, even to the point of tears.

He was not a perfect parent, but it is clear from Roosevelt's life and writings that family was very important to him. Late in life, as he sat down to write his autobiography, he reflected on his priorities:

> There are many kinds of success in life worth having. It is exceedingly interesting and attractive to be a successful business man, or railroad man, or farmer, or a successful lawyer or doctor; or a writer, or a President, or a ranchman, or the colonel of a fighting regiment, or to kill grizzly bears and lions. But for unflagging interest and enjoyment, a household of children, if things go reasonably well, certainly makes all other forms of success and achievement lose their importance by comparison.[23]

~

IN THE FALL OF 1887, shortly after Ted was born, Theodore planned another hunting trip to his beloved Badlands. He was in for a surprise, however, when he arrived with his rifle. To his utter amazement, the fabled big game of the West—deer, elk, grizzly bear, bighorn and pronghorn sheep—were few and far between. Indeed, they had vanished from large tracts of land, and the trends for the other areas where they were clinging to existence looked grim.

Theodore was now confronted with countryside almost devoid of plant and animal life. Ponds were polluted, fish and birds were dying, and fields that had once been lush were on the verge of becoming deserts. He knew something must be done. He owed it to himself, to other responsible hunters, and to his young sons, whom Theodore assumed would grow up to be hunters too.

Still thinking about the devastation he had witnessed in the Badlands, Theodore returned to New York in December, where he almost immediately called together twelve rich and powerful friends and animal lovers at his home. One prominent person at the dinner was George Bird Grinnell, editor of *Forest and Stream* magazine, an advocate for responsible hunting practices. Like Theodore, Grinnell was a moderate who valued the American hunting tradition, yet decried the senseless killing of animals in the West.

By January 1888 Theodore and his twelve dinner guests had formed the Boone & Crockett Club, which was named after American woodsmen Daniel Boone and Davy Crockett. Its express purpose was to "work for the preservation of the large game of this country, further legislation for that purpose, and assist in enforcing existing laws."[24] Roosevelt was club president until 1894, and during that time the group swelled to ninety members—including prominent lawyers, politicians, and scientists—who wielded influence that was greatly disproportionate to their numbers.

The club successfully agitated for the creation of the National Zoo in Washington, D.C., and they worked with the secretary of the interior to pass the Park Protection Act of 1894, which led to the clean-up and beautification of Yellowstone National Park. They also spear-headed efforts to safeguard the giant sequoia trees in California, build zoological gardens in New York, and create an animal refuge in Alaska. The popularity of the Boone & Crockett Club spread, and chapters were founded in England and elsewhere. The group still operates today.[25]

Theodore's concerns about the health of the natural world were not limited to animal life. He was also concerned about deforestation, and his Boone & Crockett Club joined forces with the American Forestry Association and other groups to slow the clearing of forests in the West. As a result of their lobbying, Congress passed the Forest Reserve Act of 1891, which gave the president the power to put any wooded parts of the country under federal oversight. Roosevelt used these powers to their fullest when he became president.

CHAPTER NINE

Cleaning Up the System

IN DECEMBER 1887, when Theodore was occupied with writing and conservationism, President Cleveland announced that he was lowering tariffs, the taxes on goods coming into the United States. Republicans charged that Cleveland was jeopardizing American prosperity by allowing foreign competition with more expensive American products. Large corporations favored the high tariff, and they were eager to support the Republican candidate in the presidential race of 1888.

As the issue heated up, Roosevelt told a friend that he was content with his life as a writer. "I'm a literary feller, not a politician these days," he said.[1] But when the Republicans chose Benjamin Harrison, the grandson of former president William Henry Harrison—and not James Blaine—as their candidate, Theodore agreed to make speeches on Harrison's behalf, attacking Cleveland and defending the tariffs, which had been in place since the Civil War.

Harrison won the election of 1888, but probably only because his supporters bought votes in critical states like New York and Indiana. In Pennsylvania, votes were sold for $15 in gold or $20 in currency. Still, the election was close. Harrison lost the popular vote, but won 233 electoral college votes to Cleveland's 168.

Theodore's stumping on the campaign trail had given him a renewed taste for politics. His chances of finding work in the Harrison administration were slim, however. Harrison's right-hand man was none other than James Blaine, whom Roosevelt had called corrupt in past years.

Thanks to support from powerful political friends such as Henry Cabot Lodge, Theodore was finally offered a job as one of the three United States Civil Service commissioners. The Civil Service Commission was created in 1883 to make sure that those applying for government jobs would be treated equally before the law. However, many qualified people continued to be denied jobs because civil servants were bribed to hire or promote less-qualified candidates.

Theodore began work in Washington on May 13, 1889, nine days after Harrison's inauguration. He announced that he was ready to take on corruption in government, no matter how unpopular it made him. For the next six years, the Civil Service Commission was a beehive of anti-corruption activity. Theodore investigated rumors of fraud, holding hearings when needed. In addition to reports and speeches, he wrote articles about the need for reform in government. He also asked reformers to bring cases of fraud to the attention of the commission. As he observed Roosevelt, President Harrison remarked that Theodore "wanted to put an end to all the evil in the world between sunrise and sunset."[2]

Roosevelt was convinced that the "spoils system" of job preference—where those loyal to those in charge were given jobs, and the others removed—was corrupt and needed to be replaced by a merit-based system. During his time as a civil service commissioner, 26,000 government jobs became merit-based, and for the first time women were given an equal opportunity to compete for positions.

Theodore fought to revise civil service exams so that they would better locate the most qualified applicants. He helped stamp out corruption in the New York Customs House, where the local examiners leaked questions for civil service tests in exchange for cash. He also went west to root out corruption in the postal systems of Indianapolis, Milwaukee, Chicago, and Grand Rapids. Unlike many previous commissioners who overlooked evidence of corruption, Theodore was able to say, "I have made this commission a living force."[3]

While the press cheered these efforts at reform, those who profited from the existing system opposed TR and demanded that the president fire him. Harrison stood firm, even though he didn't believe Roosevelt should be so zealous. "It is to Harrison's credit, all that we are doing to enforce the law," Theodore said. "I am part of the Administration; if I do good work it redounds to the credit of the Administration."[4]

∼

AFTER KERMIT was born in October 1889, the Roosevelt family moved into a modest home in Washington, D.C. There Theodore and Edith had tea parties and Sunday evening suppers for guests. Theodore entertained visitors with thrilling stories about his time as a cattle rancher in the Badlands. All the while, too, he kept up with his crusade for conservation.

Living in the nation's capital gave the ever-inquisitive Roosevelt a chance to rub shoulders with academics and other intellectuals on a regular basis, an opportunity he capitalized upon with relish. And when Theodore went to visit friends such as the historian Henry Adams on Lafayette Square, he had to walk past the White House. Years later, Roosevelt recalled that this walk would get his heart pounding with excitement as he dreamed about one day becoming president. At age thirty-one, he was still too young to run for the nation's highest office, but that didn't stop him from looking down the corridors of time into the not-so-distant future.

Another child, Ethel, was born to the Roosevelts on August 13, 1891, less than two weeks before Thomas Edison received a patent for his motion picture camera. With another mouth to feed, friends began to express anger and concern about the family's finances. Now with four children, Edith was forced to get a handle on the family's spending. Washington was getting more expensive all the time. Then there was need to keep up the summer home at Sagamore Hill. "The trouble," Theodore wrote sheepishly, "is that my career has been a very pleasant, honorable and useful career for a man of means, but not the right career for a man without the means."[5]

In addition to the fact that his job didn't pay very well, Theodore was getting bored with the civil service. But in 1893 the nation was firmly in the grip of a severe economic depression. It had begun because of uncertainty about the federal government's ability to support its paper currency with gold reserves. The country's currency was backed by gold and silver reserves, but Congress had passed the Silver Purchase Act of 1890 that mandated four and a half million ounces of silver to be purchased by the government each year. Because more silver was being mined to meet the government demand, its price began to fall, and a silver dollar soon became worth only fifty-three cents. Banks and other nongovernment creditors demanded repayment in gold, which was worth nearly twice as much as silver. Meanwhile, large amounts of gold were flowing out of the Treasury as nervous overseas investors expected a financial crisis. The currency, now backed largely by the silver that remained, became unstable, and the resulting inflation caused the prices of consumer goods to skyrocket. To bring the country back to a gold standard, President Cleveland managed to get Congress to repeal the Silver Purchase Act in August, but by then the damage was done. By the winter, four million Americans (out of a population of about seventy-five million) were out of work, some 600 banks had closed, and 15,000 businesses had failed.

About the only bright spot at the time was the 1893 Chicago World's Columbian Exposition. Twenty-seven million people paid fifty cents each to look back upon the 400 years of America's past since the arrival of Columbus, and to get a glimpse at what lay ahead. The message was one of optimism that America's meteoric rise would continue unabated. Massive buildings—200 in all—were constructed in the latest architectural styles; fireworks lit the night sky; and the world's first Ferris wheel took ecstatic visitors 250 feet into the sky. One fairgoer, L. Frank Baum, gained inspiration for the Emerald City, the backdrop for his 1900 masterpiece, *The Wonderful Wizard of Oz*. In addition, well-known foods such as shredded wheat, Aunt Jemima syrup, and Juicy Fruit gum, made their debut at the fair. Despite its brilliance, however, the fair could hardly disguise the fact that a hundred thousand men in Chicago were out of work.

It was against such a gloomy economic backdrop that Edith convinced Theodore to stay put until a job came along that offered a larger salary. Reluctantly, he agreed. He was in debt to the tune of almost $3,000, thanks largely to his relatively meager salary and to losses from his ill-fated ranching operation. With few other options remaining, he was reduced to selling six acres of property at Sagamore Hill, at the then-princely sum of $400 per acre, to help make up the deficit. But he knew that things could not go on this way. Adding to his anguish was the premature death of his brother, Elliott, who died in 1894 after a long bout with alcoholism.

In time, the dark economic clouds did begin to part. After six years as a civil service commissioner, Theodore was finally given a chance to change jobs. When a Republican reformist businessman named William L. Strong became mayor of New York in April 1895, Theodore was offered a seat on the New York City Board of Police Commissioners. He accepted.

Looking back near the end of his life, Roosevelt discussed his role as one of the four commissioners: "I was appointed with the distinct understanding that I was to administer the Police Department with entire disregard of partisan politics, and only from the standpoint of a good citizen interested in promoting the welfare of all good citizens. My task, therefore, was really simple."[6] Also, he noted, "there were two sides to the work: first, the actual handling of the Police Department; second, using my position to help in making the city a better place in which to live and work for those to whom the conditions of life and labor were hardest."[7]

As Theodore saw it, his most important job was to root out corruption in the police department. It was an extremely difficult task because the corruption was so widespread. Jobs in the police force, as well as promotions, came about largely through cash payoffs. Gambling and prostitution were thriving businesses in New York City because the police at all levels took bribes and looked the other way.

On May 8, 1895, Theodore's first day as a police commissioner, he

As a police commissioner in New York, Roosevelt rooted
out corruption, often roaming the streets at night to find
evil-doers and malingerers. *Theodore Roosevelt Collection,
Harvard College Library*

immediately had himself elected president of the new board. For the
next two years, Roosevelt's name was splashed across the state's newspapers as he earned the trust of reformers and the scorn of corrupt
policemen, bar owners, and some fellow Republicans. "I don't care
who the other Commissioners are," wrote his friend, the social
reformer Jacob Riis. "TR is enough."[8] As Theodore told his sister,

Bamie, "I hold the most important and corrupt department in New York in my hands. I shall speedily assail some of the ablest, shrewdest men in this city, who will be fighting for their lives, and I know how hard the task ahead of me is. Yet in spite of all the nervous strain and worry, I am glad I undertook it; for it is a man's work."[9]

Under TR's determined leadership, the police board fired New York's leading officer, police superintendent Thomas F. Byrnes. He had accumulated a personal fortune of $350,000, mostly through corruption. Other officers who took bribes from gamblers, saloonkeepers, brothel owners, and criminals were also fired. Street officers who were not found to be corrupt were given pay raises and promotions. In an age before cars, Roosevelt equipped patrolmen with bicycles, then very much in vogue, so that law enforcement would be better able to chase down those rapscallions who made their getaway on two wheels.

Theodore was a member of the police board for less than two years, but he helped turn the department into a more professional organization. As Roosevelt recalled, "We paid not the slightest attention to a man's politics or creed, or where he was born, so long as he was an American citizen; and on an average we obtained far and away the best men that had ever come into the Police Department."[10] He reduced political influence on police matters, trained the officers in using pistols, began a motorcycle patrol, widened the use of special crime units, instituted the civil service, gave women more job opportunities, opened a police academy for trainees, and introduced the telephone, horse-drawn patrol wagons, and standardized police weapons to the force.

Roosevelt's passion for his work was evident to friends and enemies alike. A police captain described TR's influence on the department:

He put new morale into the Force. All payments for advancement stopped at once. No political boss could appoint, promote, or injure you. Promotions were strictly on the level. No man was afraid to do his duty while Roosevelt was commissioner, because he knew that the commissioner was behind him. The crooks were afraid of the cops—and the cops were not afraid of the crooks. All the decent, manly fellows on the Force

loved this strenuous master who led them. He was human. You could talk
to him. He made even people with a shady past feel at home with him.[11]

TR often worked ten to twelve hours a day at his job. Late at night,
he liked to walk the streets of New York in a black trench coat with a
hat pulled over his eyes, looking for evidence of crime or police sleeping on the job. Roosevelt caught many officers loafing, and he fined or
reprimanded the offenders. Because all that could be seen of Theodore
at night were his large white teeth, some street vendors sold whistles
shaped like "Teddy's Teeth," which some surly New Yorkers blew at
police officers. (Although others referred to Roosevelt as "Teddy," he
disliked the nickname because Alice had used it, and after her death it
conjured up unpleasant memories.)

With the strong support of the city's churches, Theodore also
enforced the law making it illegal for saloons to sell alcohol on Sunday,
although he personally hoped that the State Assembly would repeal the
law. His efforts were very unpopular, and some called him "King
Roosevelt I" for allegedly setting up a dictatorship as police commissioner. There were even death threats, which TR brushed off. Once
again, however, he had developed a good relationship with the New
York City newspaper reporters, and he used them to his advantage. He
provided them with a steady stream of insider news, while they helped
him expose instances of corruption. Roosevelt's reforms also attracted
the attention of the out-of-town press, and many praised his honesty
and tenacity.

During this time, Roosevelt was also a member of the New York
City Board of Health. In that capacity, he sought to better the living
conditions of the city's less fortunate. He believed that a combination
of government action and private charity would help pull many out of
lives ruled by poverty and despair.

There was ample evidence that poverty, disease, and crime were on
the rise in his beloved city. For several decades, social reformers such
as Jacob Riis had been documenting in words and photographs the desperate conditions in which the poor of New York City lived. The recent

invention of flash powder allowed Riis and others to take photographs at night and indoors; when these pictures of grim and desperate people were published, the conscience of a city was pricked.

In his seminal work, *How the Other Half Lives* (1890), Riis wrote that the plight of the poor, long ignored by wealthy and influential New Yorkers, was now receiving much greater attention because it posed a threat to the existing social order. "There came a time," Riis wrote, "when the discomfort and crowding . . . were so great, and the consequent upheavals so violent, that it was no longer an easy thing to do, and then the upper half [of society] fell to inquiring what was the matter."[12]

Riis and others noted that European immigration to New York had skyrocketed in the last half of the nineteenth century, making the city the most densely populated in the world. He argued that this increased density, combined with squalid living conditions, had led to a sharp rise in drunkenness, disease, and crime. Riis noted that 1.2 million people, or three-fourths of the city's population, were living in tenement houses. These desperately overcrowded homes had inadequate sanitation, lighting, and ventilation. With tuberculosis rates at 38 percent,

> they are the hot-beds of the epidemics that carry death to rich and poor alike; the nurseries of pauperism and crime that fill our jails and police courts; that throw off a scum of forty thousand human wrecks to the island asylums and workhouses year by year; that turned out in the last eight years a round half million beggars to prey upon our charities; that maintain a standing army of ten thousand tramps with all that that implies; because, above all, they touch the family life with deadly moral contagion.[13]

Through their efforts to eliminate poverty and disease, Roosevelt and Riis became good friends. Roosevelt, in fact, described Riis as "the best American I ever knew, although he was already a young man when he came hither from Denmark."[14] In his autobiography, Roosevelt summarized his efforts to put into practice the suggestions of Riis and others to improve the lot of the city's poor:

New York's Hester Street, shown here in 1903, bustled with immigrants looking for a toehold in the new society. Theodore was determined to improve conditions for the less fortunate, and ensure opportunities for all. *National Archives*

> As a member of the Health Board I was brought into very close relations with the conditions of life in the tenement-house districts . . . It was largely this personal experience that enabled me . . . to struggle not only zealously, but with reasonable efficiency and success, to improve conditions. We did our share in making forward strides in the matter of housing the working people of the city with some regard to decency and comfort.[15]

In response to the exposé of the slums, the city of New York enacted the Tenement House Law of 1901, which mandated that all tenement houses built after passage of the law had to have a certain minimum room size and a minimum of light and ventilation. The New York State Tenement House commission, created in 1900, oversaw existing housing units. These reforms met with success. By 1915, the city's death rate had dropped from 19.9 per thousand to 13.53 per thousand.

Throughout his political career, Roosevelt continued to keep a close eye on the plight of the less fortunate in society. He believed strongly that it was government's responsibility to ensure that all its citizens were given an equal opportunity to be successful in life, however that was defined by the individual.

∾

BECAUSE OF THE attention Theodore was receiving, his friend Henry Cabot Lodge began to believe that Roosevelt might one day become president. In August 1895 Lodge wrote to him, "You are rushing so rapidly to the front, that the day is not far distant when you will come into a large kingdom."[16] When TR was asked by reporters if he was considering running for president, he shouted, "Don't ask me that! Don't you put such ideas in my head."[17]

CHAPTER TEN

America at War

IN THE SUMMER of 1896, William McKinley, a longtime Republican insider and governor of Ohio, won his party's presidential nomination. Thirty-six-year-old William Jennings Bryan, the editor of the *Omaha World-Herald* and a respected orator, won the Democratic Party's nomination. The election, as Bryan saw it, was about the declining standard of living of working people, and his solution was to have the federal government take steps to put more money in their hands. Bryan also believed that if the silver in the U.S. Treasury was minted, instead of gold, working men and women would have access to cheaper money. In the process, "Big business," which held many of the existing gold dollars, would be cut down to size as the value of those dollars was reduced.

The head of the Republican Party, Mark Hanna, would not sit idly by and watch Bryan walk off with the presidency. Through his connections with the nation's elite railroads, banks, insurance companies, and others, he amassed a war chest of over three and a half millions dollars that he used to print 120 million pieces of campaign literature and hire 1,400 Republican campaign speakers. The Republicans played to the popular perception that Bryan was a political radical and opponent of capitalism. Theodore Roosevelt echoed these sentiments: "[Bryan's] utterances are as criminal as they are wildly silly. All the ugly forces that seethe beneath the social crust are behind him."[1]

Roosevelt, meanwhile, was growing tired of his post as New York City police commissioner, and he began to set his sights on a bigger prize—assistant secretary of the navy. The job was ideal for Roosevelt, who had a long fascination with naval affairs, but he knew that the first step to Washington would have to be a strong show of public support for McKinley in the presidential campaign. Although he was not fond of the candidate, and had privately written Lodge that "[i]t will be a great misfortune to have McKinley nominated"[2] for president, Roosevelt was politically savvy enough to know that McKinley alone was the man who could make his political dreams a reality.

Theodore began to lay the groundwork. He lobbied friends and financial supporters of McKinley, including the boss Mark Hanna, urging them to put in a good word for him. Roosevelt himself went on the campaign trail, stumping for McKinley in a number of key states. While the candidate stayed at home and waged a "front porch" campaign with carefully prepared and rehearsed speeches, Roosevelt spoke with his trademark fire and zeal. In matching Bryan's popular appeal, TR helped to put out some potentially dangerous political fires in America's heartland. Yet he showed an unpleasant side of his political personality in these pro-McKinley speeches, likening Bryan and his running mate, John P. Altgeld, to the murderers of the French Revolution. He refused to even meet Altgeld because "I may at any time be called upon to meet the man sword to sword on the field of battle." As a dangerous revolutionary, Roosevelt believed, Altgeld and other like-minded leaders would only be stopped by "standing them against a wall, and shooting them dead. I believe it will come to that. These leaders are plotting a social revolution and the subversion of the American Republic."[3]

Despite the worries of Roosevelt and some others that Bryan posed a formidable challenge, the election results were lopsided. McKinley won easily, scoring the biggest electoral college victory of any president since 1872. Republicans retained control of the House of Representatives and won control of the Senate, thereby giving them

In this cartoon, called "Approaching Nebraska,"
Roosevelt's whirlwind campaign figured as William
Jennings Bryan's worst nightmare.

control of Congress and the White House. Bryan was gracious in
defeat, and Americans knew that they had not heard the last of him.
Bryan would go on to receive the Democratic presidential nomina-
tions in 1900, 1904, and 1908, but he never became president. In
1925, aged and infirm, he was publicly humiliated by defense attorney
Clarence Darrow for his defense of creationism in the famous Scopes
"monkey" trial.

Roosevelt was hopeful that McKinley would reward his hard work
with the naval post, but the new president was hesitant. Roosevelt had
a reputation as a reformer who liked to shake things up, and McKinley
wanted peace. Finally, after Theodore's friends in Washington lobbied

McKinley, he somewhat reluctantly sent TR's name to the Senate for confirmation. He was quickly confirmed, and began work as assistant secretary of the navy on April 19. Theodore was the first of no less than five Roosevelts, including his son Ted, to hold this office up through 1936.

His first order of business, Roosevelt believed, should be to boost the morale of troops and other military personnel who felt neglected by Congress and the McKinley administration. The new secretary of the navy, John D. Long, was not as knowledgeable as Theodore, and he was content to delegate many matters to his assistant. Taking full advantage of this authority, TR gave speeches in support of a strong navy, wrote reports, and inspected ships and naval bases. "My new job is exactly to my liking," he exulted.[4]

The rumor was that most senior naval officers were much more comfortable with Roosevelt than with Long. Historian and biographer William Harbaugh wrote that on a trip to a shipyard in Philadelphia to inspect the battleship *Iowa*, Roosevelt "broke the record for asking questions and surprised officers and shipbuilders alike with his evident theoretical knowledge of the construction of ships of war down to the details of bolts and rivets."[5] It wasn't long before the men in uniform began to claim Roosevelt as one of their own, even though he had not served in the armed forces.

Theodore's second important task was building up the navy. At the time Roosevelt went to Washington, the American navy lagged far behind the navies of Europe. As he had argued in his book, *The Naval War of 1812*, an inadequate navy could invite foreign aggression. Once in office, he called for the creation of a dozen new battleships and the building of a canal across Central America to enable American fleets to move quickly back and forth from the Atlantic Ocean to the Pacific. He also recommended the purchase of experimental submarines and an investigation into the prospects for manned flight. Congress, however, showed little interest in a military buildup, and only when war with Spain became a reality did Roosevelt win approval for various items of his wish list. Some Congressional leaders opposed expansion of the navy because they feared it would draw the United States into foreign wars. Instead, they argued for a fleet primarily to defend America's eastern and western shores. Roosevelt, on the other hand, insisted that improvements in military technology made it impossible for the United States to be safe "behind" the oceans. He believed that America needed modern ships to battle on the open sea. Two decades before World War I, he saw trouble coming with Germany in the Atlantic and Japan in the Pacific.

The differences between the cautious McKinley and the assertive Roosevelt soon became painfully obvious. While the McKinley administration was concerned with peace and prosperity, Roosevelt was thinking about nationalism and expansionism. While McKinley spoke of arbitration to settle conflicts, TR was polishing the cannons of war.

By the end of the nineteenth century, the western frontier of the United States was no more. So declared historian Frederick Jackson Turner in 1893. Whereas previous generations of Americans could be fueled by the dream of venturing into unknown open spaces and making a life for themselves and their families, Americans in the 1890s realized that this Golden Age had come to an end. Writers and academics mourned the loss because they believed that the frontier spirit was vital to the exercise of self-reliance, and therefore they argued that the loss of the frontier would damage the health of American democracy. "To the frontier," Turner wrote, "the American intellect owes its striking characteristics. That coarseness and strength . . . acuteness and inquisitiveness, that practical, inventive turn of mind . . . restless, nervous energy . . . that buoyancy and exuberance which comes with freedom."[6]

Before long, however, leading men such as Theodore Roosevelt came to realize that the frontier need not be confined to America's borders. The pioneering spirit that had animated earlier generations could be rekindled as America cast her glance upon other lands. He wrote to a friend in 1897, "In strict confidence . . . I should welcome almost any war, for I think this country needs one."[7] In later years, as president,

Roosevelt would expand the Monroe Doctrine of 1823, which had warned European powers against interfering with nations in the Western Hemisphere, to include the exercise of "international police power" by the United States to repair "flagrant cases of . . . wrongdoing or impotence" in Latin American nations.[8] To some observers, this sounded like a mere pretext for American imperialism.

Toward the end of 1897, Roosevelt began to have success in persuading President McKinley that the United States needed a more aggressive foreign policy. The focus of attention was the island of Cuba, just a few miles off the American coast. The Cuban people were in the midst of a bloody war with their Spanish colonizers, and the Spanish had begun herding Cuban women into concentration camps. News reports told of hundreds of Cubans dying of disease and starvation, and President McKinley himself donated $5,000 to relief efforts.

Most Americans wanted to end the suffering of the Cuban people and help them become independent. They were spurred on by the daily reports from the mass-produced "yellow"—or alarmist—newspapers about Spanish atrocities in Cuba. Like many Americans, Roosevelt was highly critical of Spain, and his patience had worn thin. Now, he wrote, was the time to go to war.

Hoping to avert a war with the United States, Spain offered the Cubans political autonomy, but the rebels held firm to their demand for complete independence. As war looked increasingly likely, riots broke out in the capital city of Havana in January 1898. The United States then intercepted a letter in which the Spanish minister in Washington was critical of President McKinley. It was clear to Spain that American sympathies were with the Cuban people.

But the one incident that more than anything else led to the war between Spain and the United States was the destruction of the 7,000–ton battleship U.S.S. *Maine* in Havana harbor on February 15. At least ostensibly, the ship had been on a "courtesy visit" to Cuba, and the captain and crew went sightseeing around the island. An explosion rocked the ship, killing 266 of the 354 men on board. Some military analysts felt that the explosion was accidental, and the *Maine's* captain recommended that the American people suspend judgment pending an investigation, but the court of public opinion in the United States quickly blamed Spanish sabotage. While he was noncommittal in public, privately Roosevelt called the event "an act of dirty treachery on the part of the Spaniards" and believed that war between the two nations was now inevitable.[9]

As the conflict with Spain drew toward a crisis point, TR was at home with his family in Oyster Bay, preparing for battle. This was his moment. Four-year-old Archie remembered watching his father standing with his face to the waters of Oyster Bay, shooting at a life-sized target attached to a nearby tree. Roosevelt had begun to raise a ragtag group of nonprofessional soldiers, and he wanted to make sure his aim was respectable when his volunteer regiment was sent into battle.

When the word spread that Roosevelt was forming a regiment, applications poured in. In all, he received 23,000 applications, but only 534 were selected.[10] They consisted of a cross-section of American society—from college students of privileged backgrounds to American Indians to cowboys and ranchers. When fifty-two-year-old "Buffalo Bill" Cody was unable to join due to contractual obligations, he sent some of his best riders and "shootists" from his Wild West show. Some of the men knew Roosevelt from their time together in the Badlands in the 1880s, but almost all were there because they admired him. Most of them wore flannel shirts and bandannas around their necks.

Despite the sinking of the *Maine*, President McKinley continued to seek a diplomatic resolution to the tensions with Spain. He even tried to buy Cuba, but Spain wouldn't sell it. Itching for battle, an angry Roosevelt accused McKinley of ambivalence. On April 9, 1898, Spain agreed to let the United States arbitrate its dispute with Cuba, but McKinley mistrusted the Spanish and finally sent a war message to Congress on April 11 which asserted Cuba's right to independence. Looking at the polls, McKinley knew most people wanted war, and the shrewd politician in him knew that giving the people what they wanted would help ensure his reelection in 1900.

Once the United States declared war on Spain—which had colonies in the Philippines and Guam, in addition to Cuba—Theodore resigned his naval office to volunteer as a lieutenant colonel of the 1st United States Volunteer Cavalry, better known as the "Rough Riders." In total, over 150,000 volunteers went to fight in Cuba—a staggering figure considering that the regular army, at 28,000 men, was only one-fifth of that number. Some historians have said that the Spanish-American War was one of the rare wars that was fought and won by amateurs.

Roosevelt was hardly a typical soldier. Nearing forty, he was horribly nearsighted and he had a wife and six children (from newborn to age fourteen) at home. McKinley and Secretary of the Navy Long begged him to stay home, but Roosevelt would have none of it. "It was," he remembered years later, "my one chance to do something for my country and for my family and my one chance to cut my little notch on the stick that stands as a measuring-rod in every family."[11]

On May 7, 1898, McKinley received word that the United States had destroyed the entire Spanish fleet in the Philippines without one American being killed. Soon thereafter, the Rough Riders went to fight. In June they landed on the beach in Cuba, with no Spaniards yet in sight. Theodore was relieved at their good fortune. He later wrote, "Five hundred resolute men could have prevented this disembarkation at very little cost to themselves."[12]

Carrying a pistol salvaged from the *Maine*, TR took command of the Rough Riders, and they began to march fifteen miles, at what some men felt was an uncomfortably rapid pace, toward the town of Santiago. Soon enough they encountered the enemy. At Las Guasimas, the Americans met up with a small group of Spanish soldiers. The Spanish were badly outnumbered, but they fought valiantly for more than two hours. In a letter to his sister, Corinne, Roosevelt related what happened:

Yesterday we struck the Spaniards and had a brisk fight for 2 ½ hours before we drove them out of their position. We lost a dozen men killed or mortally wounded, and sixty severely or slightly wounded. One man was killed as he stood beside a tree with me. Another bullet went through a tree behind which I stood and filled my eyes with bark.[13]

After a short rest, the order was given on June 30 to continue the march to Santiago. Arriving under cover of darkness, in daylight the Rough Riders found themselves between American and Spanish forces. When the shrapnel began flying, lightly wounding Roosevelt and severely injuring others, TR drove his men further along the Santiago road, between two hills—San Juan Hill and Kettle Hill. Roosevelt led forces in a charge that captured Kettle Hill, which overlooked the port city of Santiago. "We had to run to keep up with him," seventeen-year-old Rough Rider Jesse Langdon later said, "and running up Kettle Hill wasn't easy."[14] When they reached the top, the Rough Riders discovered that most of the Spanish troops were either dead or had fled.

Other American troops captured neighboring San Juan Hill and El Caney, routing Spanish forces. With the harbor at Santiago now vulnerable to American attacks, the Spanish admiral Pascual Cervera had no choice but to take his fleet out to sea. The results for the Spanish were equally disastrous—the Americans either sank or grounded the six Spanish warships, killing more than 300 men and taking 1,700 prisoner.

On July 17, with their military forces in shambles, the beleaguered Spanish surrendered and the American flag flew over Cuba for the first time. A month later, on August 12, Spain accepted a peace accord with terms very favorable to the victorious Americans: Cuba was granted independence, and Guam, Puerto Rico, and the Philippines were ceded to the United States. Not only had the United States expelled Spain from Cuba, but it had also gained a toehold in the Pacific, one that would prove invaluable in years to come when the empire of Japan grew into a global force.

Roosevelt ("the Colonel") stands front and center with the Rough Riders on Kettle Hill, 1898. *Photograph by William Dinwiddie. Library of Congress*

The United States was now the undisputed power in the Caribbean, just as Roosevelt had wanted, not to mention a rising force in the Pacific Rim. But not everyone was thrilled at this vast exercise in imperialism. The American Anti-Imperialist League—whose members included former president Grover Cleveland, novelist Mark Twain, and steel baron Andrew Carnegie—spoke out against the United States expanding its territory with the pretext of helping those suffering under oppressive foreign governments. As Mark Twain argued regarding the Philippines, "We have gone there to conquer, not to redeem."[15] Roosevelt dismissed Twain as "a vulgar old horror."[16]

From the time of the Spanish-American War, right through to the end of his political career, Theodore was dogged by anti-imperialists who believed that he had the blood of innocent people on his hands. They voiced to him at every turn their belief that American interests were best served by cultivating peaceful relationships with foreign governments, reducing the size of the American military, and not meddling in the internal affairs of foreign nations. TR disagreed.

CHAPTER ELEVEN

Governor and Vice President

THE ROUGH RIDERS arrived back in America on August 15, 1898, and Theodore Roosevelt was hailed as a national hero. He was known by many as "the most famous man in America." Proud of his military exploits, Roosevelt now preferred to be called "the Colonel." Soon he published *The Rough Riders*, his account of the Cuban campaign. He believed that he should be awarded the Medal of Honor for his exploits in the war, but his request was denied by the War Department, partly because there was no evidence for Roosevelt's claim that he and the Rough Riders had made the decisive charge up San Juan Hill. Roosevelt's bravery in battle was judged to be on no higher level than that of other officers.[1]*

Hoping to capitalize on his immense popularity, the Republican Party in New York urged TR to run for governor, which he did in November. "A curious and really unimportant fact," wrote one biographer, "is that Roosevelt was, in 1898, probably ineligible for the office of governor or even to vote in New York State."[2] Roosevelt had not been a resident of New York in the five years immediately leading up to 1898, as the state constitution required, but his opponents—perhaps because of TR's surging nationwide fame—chose not to press the issue.

---

* Over a hundred years later, after lobbying from family and the Theodore Roosevelt Association, President Bill Clinton awarded Theodore the medal posthumously.

Theodore didn't have much of a platform in his campaign except for a promise to run an honest administration. Despite his popularity and a boost from some former Rough Riders on the campaign trail, he only narrowly defeated the Democratic candidate, Judge Augustus Van Wyck, who was the brother of the mayor of New York City. "New York cares very little for war," TR lamented.[3] Out of 1.3 million votes cast, Theodore won by only 17,794. When told he was elected, Theodore was surprised: "Am I? That's bully!"[4]

AT THE TURN of the twentieth century, New York was still the most populous state in the Union, with thirty-six electoral college votes. It was also the most influential. In the eighteen years between 1881 and 1899, a New Yorker had been president for twelve of them.

As governor, Theodore saw himself as a mediator between political radicals like Socialists and Communists, and the city's big business interests. His first order of business upon taking office in January 1899 was to distance himself from the Republican boss, Senator Thomas C. Platt, who in Roosevelt's mind typified the sort of institutionalized political corruption that he was seeking to uncover and eradicate. As he stated in his First Annual Message, Roosevelt fancied himself "an independent organization man of the best type."[5]

Of getting things done in politics, Governor Roosevelt said, "I have always been fond of the West African proverb: 'Speak softly and carry a big stick; you will go far.'"[6] His friend, William Roscoe Thayer, later noted, "More than once in his later years he quoted this [proverb] to me, adding, that it was precisely because this or that Power knew that he carried a big stick, that he was enabled to speak softly with effect."[7]

In office Roosevelt supported the right of labor to organize, he improved civil service law, streamlined government, and instituted tax reform. He got legislation passed protecting the state's forests; he supported salary increases for public school teachers; and he signed billing banning the segregation of public schools by race. As governor, he fought powerful groups such as banks and big insurance companies for illegal corporate practices. He also supported bills to create an eight-hour workday for state employees, increase the number of factory inspectors, and place tighter restrictions on the tenement buildings where cigars and clothing were made.

~

IN MID-1899, Governor Roosevelt attended the first reunion of Rough Riders in Las Vegas, which was then part of the territory of New Mexico. Hundreds of his fellow volunteers joined in the celebration. Roosevelt gave a stirring speech to the throng, saying, "We are a great nation. We must show ourselves great, not only in the ways of peace, but in the preparedness for war which best insures peace."[8] The annual gatherings were so popular that they continued until 1966. The last surviving Rough Rider, Jesse Langdon, died in 1975 at age ninety-four. To his dying day, he had only fond memories of the man he knew as "the Colonel." "Men were drawn to him," Langdon would say later, "because they knew he was the right man. We'd have gone to hell with him."[9]

After the reunion, TR went on a nationwide speaking tour. He was greeted by cheering crowds wherever he went, and many people treated him as if he were already a presidential candidate in the election of 1900. Theodore certainly was thinking about the White House. According to friend and journalist William Allen White, Roosevelt's presidential ambitions began soon after he returned from Cuba in 1898: "He did not want to be governor of New York. He wanted to be president of the United States."[10] But Roosevelt knew that running against McKinley, a sitting president and fellow Republican, would hurt his political future if he lost. Talk among political insiders was that Roosevelt would continue as governor until McKinley had served out his two terms, then run for president in 1904.

Still, Roosevelt worried that waiting until 1904 would be risky. He was popular as a war hero, but he knew that the public mood was changeable. "I have never known a hurrah to endure for five years," he wrote.[11] Henry Cabot Lodge offered a solution. He encouraged Theodore to run for vice president in 1900, alongside McKinley. Roosevelt hesitated because he thought he could do more good as governor of New York: "Now, as Governor, I can achieve something, but as Vice-President I should achieve nothing. I would simply be a presiding officer, and that I should find a bore."[12] A man of Roosevelt's ambition plainly needed more intellectual stimulation. In addition, he was concerned that his large family wouldn't get along very well on the vice president's salary of $8,000 per year, which was $2,000 less than he was earning as governor.

Roosevelt was so concerned about being pushed into office that he went to Washington to tell President McKinley himself that he didn't want the job. To his embarrassment, McKinley wasn't even considering him. Privately, the president continued to believe that Roosevelt was too impetuous and unpredictable for such an honor.

Nevertheless, at the Republican National Convention in the summer of 1900, Roosevelt was chosen as vice president over McKinley's objections. Word was that Platt and other Republican operatives in New York had engineered TR's nomination to get him out of New York State politics. Reluctantly, Roosevelt threw his hat into the ring. He feared that the Democratic presidential candidate, William Jennings Bryan, would win the West in the general election unless he was on the Republican ticket.

Not everyone was happy with the selection of Roosevelt. Mark Hanna, the chairman of the Republican National Committee and Theodore's most vocal opponent in Washington, exclaimed in frustration, "Don't you realize that there's only one life between this madman and the White House?"[13] Hanna understood that Roosevelt, unlike McKinley, was less inclined to bend his knee to the powerful business and political machine that attempted to make and break political careers.

At the convention, McKinley was nominated unanimously on the first ballot, and Roosevelt cast the only vote against his own nomination for vice president. The Democrats nominated William Jennings Bryan for president once again, and therefore the campaign of 1900 strongly resembled the campaign of 1896—with the exception of Theodore Roosevelt on the Republican ticket. Bryan, a member of the American Anti-Imperialist League, campaigned on a pledge to keep the United States out of foreign wars.

Meanwhile, Roosevelt called for corporate ethics and the breaking up of illegal trusts. TR also responded to the charge of imperialism by arguing that the United States had an obligation to use its might to liberate oppressed peoples. He pointed out that the nation's goal was to free the Cuban people from Spanish oppression, not to make Cuba an American colony. In a famous campaign poster featuring McKinley and Roosevelt, McKinley was quoted as saying, "The American flag has not been planted in foreign soil to acquire more territory but for humanity's sake."[14]

Thanks in part to Roosevelt's robust stumping on the campaign trail, and the fact that the economic boom following the Spanish-American War had once again given Americans a "full dinner pail," the McKinley-Roosevelt ticket scored a convincing victory in the November general election, winning nearly 52 percent of the popular vote. They won by the largest vote margin in American history up to that point—861,459 votes.

In his swearing-in speech in March 1901, Vice President Roosevelt described America as "a young nation, already of great strength, yet whose political strength is but a forecast of the power that is to come."[15] With the sustained criticisms of Bryan, Twain, Carnegie, and the other anti-imperialists ringing in his ears, Roosevelt spoke in general terms of the responsibilities the United States would have in global affairs: "East and west we look across the two oceans toward the larger world life in which, whether we will or not, we must take an ever-increasing share."[16]

Once in office, Roosevelt soon felt like he had gone from the political frontlines to the political wilderness. "The Vice Presidency," he wrote, "is an utterly anomalous office (one which I think ought to be abolished). The man who occupies it may at any moment be every-

President William McKinley and his reluctant new vice president, who would go from "practically nothing" to the highest office in seven months. *Theodore Roosevelt Collection, Harvard College Library*

thing; but meanwhile he is practically nothing."[17] It didn't help matters that the Senate had adjourned until December. With nothing to do in Washington, Theodore returned to Sagamore Hill. To pass the time there, he wrote letters to friends and family, all the while thinking about his future. Would he study law once again? Or maybe write or teach about American history? If he knew anything, it was that the vice presidency was far too tame for his tastes.

On September 6, 1901, any plans TR was making were put on hold. When President McKinley was in Buffalo, New York, visiting the Pan American Exposition, he was shot and mortally wounded.

The exposition was an international festival designed to highlight progress in the Western Hemisphere. At a public reception, which his secretary had tried to cancel out of security concerns, McKinley began enthusiastically shaking hands with well-wishers, all the while greeting others he missed with a smile and his standard "Glad to see you." Three Secret Service agents, one more than usual, and five police detectives kept a watchful eye on the proceedings.

Shortly after four in the afternoon, as he worked the crowd, McKinley reached to shake the left hand of a young man with a pompadour haircut and dark gray suit. He was a Russian-Polish anarchist named Leon Czolgosz, and he fired two .32–caliber bullets from the revolver in his bandaged right hand into McKinley's chest from point-blank range. The president slumped to the ground, blood gushing from a gaping wound. After a second or two, stunned police and Secret Service agents pounced on Czolgosz, throwing him to the ground and then dragging him from the auditorium.*

The president was rushed to a nearby house. Roosevelt, who had been at a meeting of the Vermont Fish and Game Association in Lake Champlain that day, exclaimed "My God!" and rushed to McKinley's side. One bullet had missed entirely, but the other had done more serious damage. An operation was performed to remove one bullet but the second was never found. None of the doctors seemed aware that the president's kidney and pancreas had been damaged. Ironically, a newly invented X-ray machine, which might have found the second bullet, was on display at the exposition nearby.

After four days, McKinley's condition seemed to be improving, and on September 10 Roosevelt left his bedside to join Edith and the children at a camp in the Adirondack Mountains of New York. She had taken the children there in hopes that their colds would improve in the fresh mountain air.

Just three days later, while Roosevelt was climbing Mount

---

* After a one-day trial, Czolgosz was found guilty and was electrocuted a month later.

Tahawus, he received an urgent telegram from Albany: McKinley had taken a turn for the worse. In his autobiography, Roosevelt related what happened next:

> A day or two [after September 10] we took a long tramp through the forest, and in the afternoon I climbed Mount Tahawus. After reaching the top I had descended a few hundred feet to a shelf of land where there was a little lake, when I saw a guide coming out of the woods on our trail from below. I felt at once that he had bad news, and, sure enough, he handed me a telegram saying that the President's condition was much worse and that I must come to Buffalo immediately. It was late in the afternoon, and darkness had fallen by the time I reached the clubhouse where we were staying. It was some time afterwards before I could get a wagon to drive me out to the nearest railway station, North Creek, some forty or fifty miles distant. The roads were the ordinary wilderness roads and the night was dark. But we changed horses two or three times—when I say "we" I mean the driver and I, as there was no one else with us—and reached the station just at dawn, to learn from Mr. Loeb, who had a special train waiting, that the President was dead. That evening [September 14] I took the oath of office, in the house of Ansley Wilcox, at Buffalo.[18]

McKinley died of gangrene. Secretary of War Elihu Root, the highest-ranking member of McKinley's cabinet present at the time, immediately swore in Theodore Roosevelt as the country's twenty-sixth president. TR promised that he would "continue, absolutely unbroken, the policy of President McKinley."[19] At age forty-two, Roosevelt became the youngest president in American history. He was the fourth sitting vice president to become president after the death of the president, and the third within the past forty years.

Riding on McKinley's funeral train from Buffalo to Washington, Republican boss Mark Hanna felt that his worst nightmare had come true. "I told William McKinley it was a mistake to nominate that wild man. . . . Now look, that damned cowboy is President of the United States!"[20]

Chapter Twelve

Life in the White House

By sheer coincidence, Theodore's first day in the White House—September 23, 1901—would have been his father's seventieth birthday. Roosevelt felt it was a good sign, and he sensed his father's presence with him. He was also aware that he stood on the shoulders of presidents who had come before him, that he had inherited their great office. One in particular fascinated him: "I like to see in my mind's eye the gaunt form of Lincoln stalking through these halls," he said.[1] Lincoln was for Roosevelt a constant reminder that the cause of justice must prevail, whatever the political consequences. As Lincoln had ended racial slavery, so Roosevelt intended to end corporate slavery.

Businessmen were worried about the new president, but they soon found that he was temperamentally a moderate. He was pragmatic, and not as dogmatic as he might appear. He knew that he hadn't been elected president.

Roosevelt said he wanted to stay McKinley's course, but he was not wholly sincere. TR had grander plans in mind. He really wanted to transform the presidency and make it, not Congress, the ultimate seat of federal power. He also wanted to make the federal government the most important and decisive influence in public affairs. He wanted to dust off the "big stick" last used by President Lincoln during the Civil War and use it to beat Congress into compliance with his agenda for the nation. As one reporter observed toward the end of 1901, "I should say that he has something up his sleeve."[2] Shortly after becoming president, Roosevelt said to a friend, "I am happy, very happy: the only fly in the amber is that I am an accidental president; but I intend to be President of *all* the people."[3]

From the very beginning, it was clear that Roosevelt's style of governance was far different from that of his predecessor. While McKinley was soft-spoken and gentle in his manner, Roosevelt was explosive and direct. This came as a shock: Those in Congress, long used to wielding the real power in Washington, soon came to realize that Roosevelt intended to relocate a large portion of the power in the office of the presidency.

Theodore's initial policy moves met with stiff opposition from members of Congress, who resented him, so he found another way of getting his message across. Although he continued to meet with congressmen who wished to discuss policy issues, Roosevelt found it was more effective to appeal directly to the American people. In speaking directly to them, Theodore inspired the country with his energy and charisma.

～

THE ROOSEVELTS were finally able to enjoy public life. With the president making $50,000 a year, plus allowances for household expenses, they no longer had to worry about grinding fish meal to make tooth powder, as Edith had done earlier in Theodore's career.

Before the age of television, or even radio, Theodore was a master of publicity and public relations. Unlike his predecessors, he loved the trappings of the presidency. He entertained everyone from foreign dignitaries to novelists to artists to former Rough Riders. One old woman from Jacksonville, Florida, came to visit Roosevelt, and when she told him she just wanted to see a live president, he quipped, "That's very kind of you. Persons from up here go all the way to Florida just to see a live alligator."[4]

At the turn of the century, even in the wake of the McKinley assassination, the president's home had a more informal atmosphere than it does today. President Roosevelt thrived on meeting ordinary people at the White House and hearing their concerns. Once the president asked a young visitor, who appeared to be all alone, "What can I do for you?" According to one biographer,

> the boy told how his father had died leaving his mother with a large family and no money, and how he was selling typewriters to help support her. His mother, he said, would be most grateful if the President would accept a typewriter from her as a gift. So the President told the little fellow to go and sit down until the other visitors had passed, and then he would attend to him. No doubt, the boy left the White House well contented—and richer.[5]

On other occasions, an old friend would arrive at the White House and inform Roosevelt's secretary, Mr. Loeb, that he wished to see the president:

> To the President some persons were, of course, privileged. If an old pal from the West, or a Rough Rider came, the President did not look at the clock, or speed him away. The story goes that one morning Senator Cullom came on a matter of business and indeed rather in a hurry. On asking who was "in there," and being told that a Rough Rider had been with the President for a half-hour, the Senator said, "Then there's no hope for me," took his hat, and departed.[6]

Dinners at the White House became celebrated events in their own right. Most times there were scheduled, formal events exclusively for dignitaries and diplomats, but sometimes the guests were from very different backgrounds. The president, as usual, did what he could to help things go smoothly. That task was harder than it might seem:

> Perhaps Roosevelt himself felt a little trepidation as to how the unmixables would mix. He is reported to have said to one Western cowboy of whom he was fond: "Now, Jimmy, don't bring your gun along to-night. The British Ambassador is going to dine too, and it wouldn't do for you

to pepper the floor round his feet with bullets, in order to see a tenderfoot dance."[7]

~

THE PRESIDENT'S DAY usually began at 7:30, when he woke, bathed, shaved, and dressed in clothes laid out for him. He had breakfast—often peaches and cream and coffee with seven lumps of sugar in a cup that his son, Ted, said was "more in the nature of a bathtub"[8]—with his family at 8:00. He arrived at his desk in the White House by half-past nine, went over the day's appointments and schedule, and answered the most pressing of the 500 letters received every day. He dictated his replies to the letters in a rapid-fire style; once he dictated a 30,000–word critique of a book he had just read. He also sifted through newspaper and magazine clippings gathered for his attention; he insisted that every article about his administration be shown to him, even unfavorable ones. A staffer was instructed to go through 350 newspapers and clip stories reflecting the mood of the nation.

That done, TR received visitors from 10:00 until 1:00, when he met the press while his barber was shaving him. Theodore liked and was on a first-name basis with most of the reporters assigned to cover him. However, the president had little patience with those who reported comments he intended to be confidential. When a journalist did betray Roosevelt's trust, he was effectively banished from Roosevelt's inner circle. Critics charged the president with hypocrisy for punishing those in the media for being outspoken when he himself was the same way. Threat of ostracism firmly in mind, the media still swarmed the White House, wanting to know everything about the first family. But Theodore asked that the press leave his children alone. He was fair game, but he felt that his children's business was just that—*their* business.

Some of his children, however, welcomed the media attention, especially his oldest child, the headstrong Alice. Seventeen when her father became president, she was dubbed "Princess Alice" by the press and behaved outrageously to craft her own identity as a rising member of "society." She smoked in public, flirted with men, had a pet garter snake named Emily Spinach and a pet macaw named Eli Yale; she bet at the racetrack, and had "loose" friends. She was in many ways a forerunner of modern feminism, and she reflected the fact that the life of the cities in turn-of-the-century America was making women more independent-minded. Already four million women—teachers, secretaries, writers, nurses, and so on—were in the workforce by 1890.

Once while he was president, Alice continually interrupted a meeting between her father and a friend. TR's friend protested, "Theodore, isn't there anything you can do to control Alice?" With a glimmer in his eye, Roosevelt quipped, "I can do one of two things. I can be President of the United States or I can control Alice. I cannot do both."[9] Another time Theodore observed that Alice "only makes her appearance well after noon having been up all hours dancing the night before."[10] TR loved his daughter, but soon after he took office she turned eighteen; thanks to the funds provided by her maternal grandparents, she began to live her own life, away from the political arena. Theodore and Edith wanted her to settle down and get married, but their wishes meant little to a young woman just coming into her own.

As Alice explained years later, "There hadn't been a girl in the White House. . . . well, a grown-up one anyway . . . since Nellie Grant [in the 1870s]. So when [the press] saw me, the daughter of a very popular President, I aroused some interest. There was no Hollywood and there were no movie stars in those days. They liked my father and there I was having a good time and not really giving a damn."[11]

Alice admitted she was rebelling against "the social conventions of the day. One was never allowed out with a date and one had to go to a dance with a chaperone. . . . One could never give a man a lift [in a carriage], not even a White House aide."[12] She married Nick Longworth, a Republican congressman fourteen years her senior, on February 17, 1906. "One of the reasons I married was because I felt I had to get away from the White House and my family," Alice later recalled. "I . . . wanted a place of my own."[13]

Like her husband Theodore, Edith Roosevelt soon went to work putting her own distinct stamp on the White House. She redecorated the private living quarters with new carpet, new furniture, paintings, and new curtains. She filled the house with flowers, and sometimes she even went shopping for bargains in the city's antique and junk shops. In addition to raising five young children and coping with numerous pets, she brought order to the daily operations of the White House, directing its staff with a firmness that was tempered by grace and humor. She hosted numerous social gatherings, impressing friends and visitors with her warmth, happiness, and dignity. Even the fluctuating moods—her "good days" and "bad days"—that had plagued her in the past seem to have flattened out once she became first lady. Her husband was overflowing with admiration:

> I do not think my eyes are blinded by affection when I say that she has combined to a degree I have never seen in any other woman the power of being the best of wives and mothers, the wisest manager of the household, and at the same time the ideal great lady and mistress of the White House.[14]

The younger children, however, had free rein. Kermit and Ethel explored the streets of the capital on bikes, while the younger children walked on stilts through the cavernous rooms of the White House and roller skated in the cellars. With so many young children around, the executive mansion kept a collection of rabbits, guinea pigs, and hamsters in the basement. "Guinea pigs," Roosevelt wrote,

> were the stand-bys: their highly unemotional nature fits them for companionship with adoring but over-enthusiastic young masters and mistresses. Then there were flying squirrels, and kangaroo rats, gentle and trustful, and a badger whose temper was short but whose nature was fundamentally friendly . . . We also had a young black bear whom the children christened Jonathan Edwards . . . As for the dogs, of course there were many, and during their lives they were intimate and valued family friends, and their deaths were household tragedies.[15]

Archie and Quentin enjoyed sliding down the main White House stair-case on metal trays. Small boys popped out of vases in the East Room. Quentin once took his Shetland pony in the elevator to visit Archie, who was sick with measles, and a family parrot screeched "Hurrah for Roosevelt!"

Throughout his time in the White House, Roosevelt made his children a priority. One friend wrote:

> When the children were young, he usually saw them at supper and into bed, and he talked of the famous pillow fights they had with him. House guests at the White House some times unexpectedly caught sight of him crawling in the entry near the children's rooms, with two or three children riding on his back.[16]

Sometimes Theodore himself joined Ethel's friends for games of hide-and-seek in the attic, usually insisting on being "it." Edith was heard to comment from time to time that to be married to Theodore was like having another child. An observer agreed: "You must always remember that the President is about six."[17] According to a close friend, "The boyishness of Roosevelt was so conspicuous a trait that no one ever thought of him as other than a young man to the very day of his death."[18]

Alice, the oldest child, always had warm memories of her father. Years after his death, she wrote, "I don't suppose any parent ever participated more actively in the pastimes of his children than my father did. He seemed to be involved in everything . . . He was an incredible father and great fun. He was never mean. Well, not really mean. Just noble mean on occasion."[19]

As the twentieth century began, Americans were as enthralled as ever by sports. Men and boys cheered for baseball legends like Ty Cobb and Christy Mathewson; college football teams battled each other with abandon—and without helmets. In boxing, Jack Johnson, a black man, gained fame by defeating a string of white opponents and capturing the hearts of many young ladies.

The Roosevelt family at Sagamore Hill. From left: Quentin, Theodore, Ted Jr., Archie, Alice, Kermit, Edith, and Ethel. *Theodore Roosevelt Collection, Harvard College Library*

The man in the White House was also a boxer, as he had been since college. In late 1904, two years after leg surgery for wounds sustained during a trolley accident, Roosevelt suffered a serious injury. He was sparring in the White House with a young military officer when his opponent landed a well-placed punch to Roosevelt's left eye. Although TR tried to put the alarmed young man at ease by minimizing the extent of his injury, in time the wound led to the president losing use of that eye.

Characteristically, however, Roosevelt continued to box, in addition to taking up wrestling and judo. And he went horseback riding at every possible opportunity (sometimes with cabinet officials to escape the glare of the public eye in Washington), and he also played tennis on a newly laid-out court behind White House with close friends, whom he called his "Tennis Cabinet." Even as the president, Theodore held true to his childhood promise to "make" his body. In his vigorous athleticism, he, more than anyone else, exemplified the can-do attitude that would come to characterize the first American century.

∼

FOR SEVEN SUMMERS the summer White House was at Sagamore Hill, sovereign Roosevelt territory. There were no telephones until Roosevelt became president (previously a telephone message had to be relayed by bicycle messenger from the local drugstore), but then a person could call Oyster Bay 67 to reach TR. And once he became "Mister President," Secret Service agents began to patrol the grounds, trying—usually successfully, but sometimes not—to keep track of the president's whereabouts. Once the president managed to elude his Secret Service detail and took a thirty-mile nighttime ride on horseback before returning to Sagamore Hill. Another time he went camping overnight with only Ted, Kermit, and their cousin Philip, much to the horror of his security detail. Apart from the minor inconveniences of the telephone and the added protection, life at Sagamore Hill remained the same for the Roosevelt family. Edith was still a mother and Theodore was still a father and the children were still children. According to everyone who knew them, Ted, Kermit, Ethel, Archie, and Quentin "were just plain American kids who dressed sensibly, played sensibly, got their hands and faces dirty a dozen times a day; and didn't put on airs when they came to town."[20] Their mother made sure that the public spotlight did not weaken the bonds of family.

In July 1902, on his first trip back to Oyster Bay since becoming president, Theodore was greeted at the train station by a joyous throng of neighbors. Despite the pouring rain, Roosevelt smiled and exclaimed, "Delighted to see you!" "Well, old man, and how are you?" "Yes, I tell you, it seems good to be home again!"[21] The following Sunday, as the Roosevelt family sat in their usual place at Christ Episcopal Church, another neighbor came up to the president and asked, "Teddy, how's your woman?"[22] Theodore Roosevelt may have been the president of the rest of the country, but to his neighbors back in Oyster Bay, he was simply an old friend.

CHAPTER THIRTEEN

President Roosevelt

THE FIRST CONTROVERSY of the Roosevelt presidency took place only a month into the new administration. At one small dinner held by the Roosevelts on October 16, 1901, Booker T. Washington became the first African American to dine at the White House. Washington had visited the White House in secret on September 29, when Roosevelt asked him for advice on bringing Southern blacks and whites together. At their October dinner, the two men continued their discussion of race and politics in the South. Washington was the most prominent black leader of the time, and Roosevelt thought it wise to turn to him "for some suggestions as to appointing colored persons to offices in the South."[1]

Infuriated, many Southern whites charged the president with encouraging racial mixing and social equality for blacks. The *New Orleans Times-Democrat* asked, "White men of the South, how do you like it? When Mr. Roosevelt sits down to dinner with a Negro, he declares that the Negro is the social equal of the white man."[2] The *Memphis Scimitar* charged that Roosevelt had committed "the most damnable outrage ever perpetrated by any citizen of the United States when he invited a nigger to dine with him at the White House."[3]

Roosevelt was somewhat surprised at the criticism coming from the South. As the first president to have both Union and Confederate lineage, he was especially keen to heal old wounds and further unify the country. Indeed four days after taking office, he had told a *New York*

Roosevelt's speaking style was as energetic as his personality. Here he addresses a crowd in Maine. *Bath Historical Society, Maine*

Evening Post reporter of his desire to "see the South back in full communion" with the rest of the country. He added that in terms of getting federal posts, the black man "has nothing to fear from President Roosevelt because of his color."[4] At other times he pointed out that his mother's family had deep roots in the region, and several of his uncles had fought for the Confederate cause during the Civil War.

But Theodore was also a shrewd politician. He never invited another black leader to the White House because he knew he would need Southern votes when he ran for president in his own right in 1904.

∽

AS THE FUROR over Booker T. Washington's visit to the White House died down, a much bigger controversy engulfed the Roosevelt administration. In February 1902, the United States Justice Department filed suit to dissolve J.P. Morgan's Northern Securities Company, a giant holding company that controlled most of the western railroads, for violation of the Sherman Antitrust Act of 1890. Roosevelt believed that Morgan was not allowing other companies to compete. This was a move of considerable courage, and not only because Morgan had donated $2.1 million to Roosevelt's campaign fund.

Morgan had been a friend of Roosevelt's father, and both were founders of The American Museum of Natural History. In addition to railroads, he owned many well-known trusts, including General Electric and American Telephone & Telegraph (AT&T). His wealth and influence were so staggering that President Grover Cleveland had come to him in 1895 and asked for his help in shoring up American currency with gold reserves. (In exchange he made a tidy profit selling government bonds on the open market.) In middle age, Morgan developed a skin disease that turned his nose into a large red bulb, but his eyes were so piercing that looking into them was said to be like looking into the lights of an oncoming train. According to his son-in-law, Herbert L. Satterlee, "He was the embodiment of power and purpose."[5]

Wall Street was angered at the lawsuit, but the American people were largely supportive of the federal government. Some large corporations tried everything in their power to discredit Roosevelt. "They threw doubts, for instance, on his sanity, and one heard that the 'Wall Street magnates' employed the best alienists [psychiatrists] in the country to analyze everything the President did and said, in the hope of accumulating evidence to show that he was too unbalanced to be President."[6]

Roosevelt believed that large corporations should be sensitive to the wishes of the American people, and he believed in "good" and "bad" trusts. He subscribed to the idea that improved standards of living in America were tied to the increased productivity brought about by large corporations. For example, the boom in railroad traffic in the late nineteenth century, which led directly to cheaper products for consumers, was due in part to the fact that industrialist Andrew Carnegie's Carnegie Steel Company had devised more efficient methods of production that dropped the price of steel rails from $168 a ton in 1868 to $31 a ton in 1884. At the turn of the century, 193,368 miles of railroad tracks crisscrossed the nation. Paychecks just from Carnegie Steel's successor, U.S. Steel Corporation—which announced its formation on March 4, 1901, the day McKinley and Roosevelt were sworn in—were responsible for feeding well over a million people. By some later estimates, a full-two thirds of the nation's gross domestic product was derived from the operations of this and other trusts.[7]

Still, many shared the opinion of Mary Lease, a member of the Populist Party from Kansas:

> Wall Street owns the country. It is no longer a government of the people, by the people, and for the people, but a government of Wall Street, by Wall Street, and for Wall Street. The great common people of this country are slaves, and monopoly is the master.[8]

At the same time Roosevelt was campaigning against trusts, other reformers such as Robert La Follette, the well-known governor of Wisconsin (and later United States senator) were agitating for social reforms such a regulation of the railroads, direct primary elections, and a more equitable tax system. Roosevelt was not prepared to say that trusts were the root of all evil, but he did believe that the unethical ones needed to be brought to account. And the need for reform, he believed, was urgent: "The republic cannot live ten years longer if things go on this way."[9] Naturally, his moderate position drew scorn from all sides. Two years later, Northern Securities was broken up, and the Supreme Court, in a landmark decision, upheld the government's action by a slim five-to-four majority. TR's reputation as a "trustbuster" was established. One writer at the time commented—as it turns out optimistically—"Even Morgan no longer rules the earth, and other men may still do business without asking his permission."[10]

The momentum created by the Northern Securities case led in 1903 to the establishment of a Bureau of Corporations within the newly created Department of Commerce and Labor in the federal government. The purpose of the bureau was to keep tabs on interstate corporations and take action against those engaging in unfair monopolistic practices. The first major case brought by the bureau was against Swift & Company, the so-called "beef trust." In 1905, the Supreme Court followed the Northern Securities decision with a ruling that ordered the breakup of meatpackers Swift & Company. The court reversed an earlier decision from 1895 (*U.S. v. E. C. Knight Company*) in which they held that the Sherman Antitrust Act didn't apply to manufacturing companies.

In 1906 and 1907, the Roosevelt administration brought suit against other prominent monopolies, including the Standard Oil Company, the American Tobacco Company, and the DuPont Corporation. During Theodore's seven years in office, the Department of Commerce and Labor began antitrust cases against more than forty-five corporations. Despite these efforts, however, trusts continued to be created. A 1904 survey listed 305 trusts, or industrial corporations, with assets of over $7 billion, which was up from 185 trusts and $3 billion in assets in 1899. And thirteen more trusts, with $500 million in combined assets, were in the works.[11] After leaving the White House, it is little wonder Roosevelt conceded that, with regard to the breakup of illegal trusts, "I was able to accomplish only a small part of what I desired to accomplish."[12]

President Theodore Roosevelt "tames the Trusts" in this *Harper's Weekly* cartoon from 1904.

As the Justice Department was seeking to dissolve Northern Securities, Roosevelt faced an equally daunting challenge to the American economy. This one emanated from the anthracite (hard) coal mines of Pennsylvania, where 147,000 largely immigrant mine workers organized by the United Mine Workers of America had been on strike since May 12. As winter approached, and national coal supplies for heating were dwindling, prices skyrocketed and coal riots erupted in some northern cities.

Theodore knew that a prolonged coalminers' strike would have catastrophic results for the economy. He called George F. Baer, chief spokesman for the mine owners, and John Mitchell, president of the United Mine Workers of America, into his office. Roosevelt told the men he couldn't force them to settle the issue, but he said, "I appeal to your patriotism."[13] He argued for a "square deal" for both sides, a phrase that caught the fancy of the public.

Mitchell agreed to binding arbitration then and there, but Baer was indignant that the mine owners were being asked to negotiate with "anarchists," which is how management viewed the mine workers. Roosevelt was furious, and he informed J.P. Morgan, who was financing the mine operations, that federal forces would seize and operate the mines unless Baer had a change of heart. Morgan then pressured Baer into negotiating.

The issue that led to the strike was an insistence by the United Mine Workers that they be paid a living wage in exchange for working in extremely hazardous day-to-day conditions. The average miner earned $560 a year. Their demands were a 10 to 20 percent pay raise, an eight-hour workday, and corporate recognition of the miners' union. Six railroad owners, who controlled as much as 80 percent of the anthracite fields, had refused to meet those demands.

When the two sides agreed to binding arbitration, the miners went back to work, and a national disaster was averted. A commission set up to mediate the dispute decided on March 22, 1903 that the mine workers would be awarded a 10 percent pay raise and a workday reduced to nine or ten hours. Mine owners would not recognize the union, however, and coal prices would be raised 10 percent.

Roosevelt's stance toward the unions straddled a fine line. On one hand, he favored the right of workers to unionize, but he deplored abuses perpetrated by union bosses. He was also opposed to work stoppages and the intervention of labor unions in politics. Roosevelt was not sympathetic to corporations abusing the rights of workers, but he was afraid of the general anarchy, or lawlessness, that could arise when disgruntled workers used violence to achieve their objectives. "If ever anarchy is triumphant," he said, "its triumph will last but for one red moment, to be succeeded for ages by the gloomy night of despotism."[14]

And so the president steered a middle course in his dealings with unions. He sent federal troops into Arizona in 1903 and Nevada in 1908 to put down union disturbances at other mines, but he also wrote in 1904, "I would guarantee by every means in my power the right of laboring men to join a union, and their right to work as union men without illegal interference from either capitalists or nonunion men."[15] With the resolution of the anthracite coal miners' strike, Roosevelt set precedents by being the first president to intervene in a labor dispute, propose binding arbitration, and threaten to use troops to seize a strike-bound industry.

One battle against "the Trusts," as they were called, may have been won, but Roosevelt believed that the coal strike was a watershed in American labor history. He argued that it signaled the rise of national corporations and the decline in influence of small "mom and pop" businesses:

> The old familiar, intimate relations between employer and employee were passing. A few generations before, the boss had known every man in his shop; he called his men Bill, Tom, Dick, John; he inquired after their wives and babies; he swapped jokes and stories and perhaps a bit of tobacco with them. In the small establishment there had been a friendly human relationship between employer and employee.
>
> There was no such relation between the great railway magnates, who controlled the anthracite industry, and the one hundred and fifty thousand men who worked in their mines, or the half million women and children who were dependent upon these miners for their daily bread . . . Again, a few generations ago an American workman could have saved money, gone West and taken up a homestead. Now the free lands were gone. In earlier days a man who began with pick and shovel might have

come to own a mine. That outlet too was now closed, as regards the immense majority, and few, if any, of the one hundred and fifty thousand mine workers could ever aspire to enter the small circle of men who held in their grasp the great anthracite industry. The majority of the men who earned wages in the coal industry, if they wished to progress at all, were compelled to progress not by ceasing to be wage-earners, but by improving the conditions under which all the wage-earners in all the industries of the country lived and worked, as well, of course, as improving their own individual efficiency.[16]

Despite the fact that the United States continued to struggle with concentrations of power and money, the American economy grew during the Roosevelt years. After 1907, the nation's gross national product reached $50 billion.

~

AFTER SUCCESSFULLY brokering a deal that ended the coal strike, Theodore headed for the banks of the Little Sunflower River in Mississippi to do some bear hunting. He could hardly have picked a place where he was more unpopular. The majority white population was still seething over his White House dinner with Booker T. Washington, and now he had just appointed the first ever African American to a high federal office: Dr. William D. Crum, Collector of Customs at the port of Charleston, South Carolina. Roosevelt understood the charged political atmosphere, and he went to great lengths to keep the location of his trip secret. He did not want to be the second president assassinated in as many years.

The president's luck was horrible. Not a bear was to be seen for five days. Then came news that a member of his party had captured a black bear. Roosevelt rushed to the site, where he found a bear cub tied to a tree. The bear weighed only 235 pounds, and it was bloodied from battle with hunting dogs and the butt of one of the party's guns. Roosevelt took pity on the cub and refused to shoot it, although he had to put it out of its misery later.

Roosevelt's kindness toward the cub drew national attention. Cartoonists depicted the scene for millions of curious readers, and soon "Teddy" bears began to roll off production lines and onto the shelves of toy stores. Roosevelt's name—the nickname he detested—would be attached to one of the most enduring toys of all time.

∼

EVEN BEFORE HE went into politics, TR's love of nature made him something of a conservationist. From boyhood on, he spent as much time as possible outdoors. Being close to nature seemed to invigorate him, to lift his spirits as nothing else could, and he greatly desired to pass that legacy on to his own children, as well as to all Americans. "This was a genuine feeling and not a political ploy," remarked his daughter Alice.[17]

Roosevelt was not content to simply admire nature, however. He knew that if America's natural resources were to be enjoyed by subsequent generations, the federal government must intervene in their governance. As he wrote in his 1905 book, *Outdoor Pastimes of an American Hunter,*

> There can be nothing in the world more graceful than the Yosemite, the groves of giant sequoias, the Canyon of Colorado, the Canyon of the Yellowstone, the Three Tetons; and our people should see to it that they are preserved for their children and their children's children forever, with their majestic beauty all unmarred.[18]

The crusade to save America's natural beauty was an extension of Roosevelt's crusade against the excesses of big business. He could not and would not tolerate the essential greed and selfishness that stood behind both the oppression of the laborer and the wanton destruction of nature. He had learned firsthand in the Dakota Territory the importance of striking a balance between the forces of industry and the forces of nature—and the tragic consequences that often result when humans are given unfettered access to natural resources. By the time Roosevelt went hunting in the Badlands in 1887, for example, he found to his horror that most of the buffalo and large game had been eradicated due to indiscriminate hunting. An estimated five million buffalo had been slaughtered between 1867, when the Union Pacific Railroad first crossed through the Dakota Territory, and 1887.

As president, the steps Roosevelt took to preserve the natural environment of the United States were not easy. As he later wrote, "The idea that our natural resources were inexhaustible still obtained, and there was as yet no real knowledge of their extent and condition."[19] Roosevelt believed that Americans must make wise use of the natural resources of their land and stop their destruction. He argued that conserving natural resources must be a fundamental objective of American domestic policy. Other politicians before him had spearheaded some limited work in conservation, but Roosevelt, with his typical blend of zeal and idealism, raised the public profile of conservation and took it giant leaps forward.

President Roosevelt was not a conservationist such as we might know today. He would not have been comfortable saying, as some leading environmentalists do, that capitalism lies at the heart of environmental destruction. Rather than close off natural resources to human use by nationalizing them (as some in his day desired), Roosevelt believed that a mixture of free market capitalism and governmental regulation offered the best way forward. To that end, he allowed logging companies to chop down forests for lumber, western lands to be opened to grazing, and rivers to be dammed for irrigation and electrical power. Roosevelt believed that corporations sometimes managed natural resources wisely—or could be taught how to—and he refused to tar them all with a broad brush. "Forest protection," TR told Congress, "is not an end of itself; it is a means to increase and sustain the resources of our country and the industries which depend on them."[20]

Roosevelt was greatly aided in his understanding of conservation issues by Gifford Pinchot. A confidant of the president, Pinchot was chosen in 1905 as the first head of the United States Forest Agency, an agency that operated within the U.S. Department of Agriculture's Division of Forestry. It was Pinchot who first told the president that, at the present rate of destruction, there would only be enough timber to last another twenty or thirty years.

Roosevelt secured passage of a number of landmark bills designed to conserve the environment. In 1902, TR signed the Reclamation Act, which gave Washington the right to build structures to alleviate flooding and drought in western lands primarily owned by the federal government. One drought-stricken area was the Salt River Valley of Arizona, which flourished after the building of the Roosevelt Dam, leading to a population boom in cities such as Phoenix.

Before logging interests persuaded Congress to amend the 1891 law allowing presidents broad discretion to declare areas as "forest preserves" or national forests, Roosevelt added 148 million acres to the nation's national forest preserve. As one observer noted, however, his move was not popular with everyone:

> The long-standing practice of stealing these lands was checked and put a stop to as rapidly as possible. Individuals and private companies had bought for a song great tracts of national property, getting thereby, it might be, the title to mineral deposits worth fabulous sums; and these persons were naturally angry at being deprived of the immense fortunes which they had counted on for themselves.[21]

In June 1903, through executive order, Roosevelt established the Pelican Island Federal Wildlife Refuge. Established on federally owned land in Florida to protect egrets and other birds from plume hunters who wanted feathers for fashionable women's hats, it was the first of fifty federal bird reservations created by Roosevelt. Among the other birds that came at least partially under government protection in various bird sanctuaries were terns, cormorants, and puffins.

By the time Roosevelt became president, the federal government had already created five national parks—Yellowstone (1872), Yosemite (1890), Sequoia (1890), General Grant (1890)—which was incorporated into Kings Canyon National Park in 1940—and Mount Rainier (1899). Theodore added five more: Crater Lake in Oregon; Wind Cave in South Dakota; Sully Hill in North Dakota; Platt in Oklahoma; and Mesa Verde in Colorado. He also pushed through Congress $15 million in new appropriations to restore decimated buffalo herds in Yellowstone. Five years later, on June 8, 1906, Roosevelt signed the National Monuments Act, which gave the president the right to have landmarks on federal lands declared national monuments. During his presidency, Roosevelt created a total of eighteen national monuments, including Holy Cross and Montezuma, Colorado; Olympic Forest, Mount Rainier, Mount Olympus, and Cascade, Washington; Bear Lodge, Wyoming; Big Belt, Big Hole, and Otter Forest, Montana; Toiyabe, Nevada; Petrified Forest and Grand Canyon, Arizona; and Blue Mountain, Oregon.

The 230 million acres he added to federal lands quadrupled the existing acreage. In 1932, as a testament to Theodore Roosevelt, the Medicine Bow Forest Preserve in Wyoming and Colorado, which Roosevelt had formed in 1905, was renamed Roosevelt National Forest. The 110–square-mile Theodore Roosevelt National Park, located in the Badlands near Medora, North Dakota, was created in 1947 to honor Roosevelt as a conservationist president.

≈

IN FOREIGN AFFAIRS, the president believed that he should "speak softly and carry a big stick." At the beginning of the twentieth century, America was not the superpower it is today. Roosevelt was anxious to demonstrate that the United States could be just as powerful politically and militarily on the world stage as it had shown itself to be economically.

One of the first orders of business for Roosevelt was tidying up some loose ends left after the end of the Spanish-American War of 1898. Cuba became an American protectorate in 1902 when the United States military forces, which had been occupying the island, withdrew. The United States also installed an effective civilian government in place in the Philippines and placed that nation under American oversight until the people could govern themselves.

As an advocate for a strong navy, Roosevelt built more ships, and established naval bases in Cuba and the Philippines. In 1901, the United States ranked fifth in the world in naval power; by 1907, it was second only behind Britain. While keeping an eye on Japan's military buildup in the Pacific, Roosevelt knew that the German threat was much more worrisome for the United States; thus the American naval presence was particularly prominent in the Atlantic. With the rise of Japan as a major power, however, Roosevelt put plans in motion to build a permanent center of American naval operations in the Pacific, at Pearl Harbor in Hawaii.

Roosevelt's foreign policy was dictated more by strategic national security interests than economic ones. He wanted powerful nations like the United States to police the world. He believed that this was necessary because the fortunes of the developed and developing countries were becoming increasingly interconnected. In a speech delivered in May 1907, Roosevelt spoke of two simultaneous objectives of the American government—to play "an ever growing part in the affairs of the world" and at home "to strive measurably to realize certain ideals."[22] The enhanced American global military presence put teeth in Roosevelt's proposed police operations.

Perhaps Roosevelt's most noteworthy foreign policy achievement was the building of the Panama Canal. It had been the dream of many to build a waterway across the narrow strip of Central America to allow ships to pass through without having to go around the tip of South America. The financial benefits to corporations and consumers were obvious. According to others, building the canal was also a matter of national security:

> The ship-canal talked about as a probability in 1850 had become a necessity by 1900. During the Spanish-American War, the American battleship *Oregon* had been obliged to make the voyage around [South America's]

The President was a political cartoonist's delight, and not all of them saw him as the savior of the world. Top, an anti-imperialist cartoon criticizes TR; bottom, an ambiguous double view.

Cape Horn, from San Francisco to Cuba, and this served to impress on the people of the United States the really acute need of a canal across the Isthmus, so that in time of war with a powerful enemy, our Atlantic fleet and our Pacific fleet might quickly pass from one coast to another. It would obviously be impossible for us to play the role of a World Power unless we had this short line of communication.[23]

The French had tried unsuccessfully to build a canal across Panama in 1889, but in 1900 the Republican Party officially supported the Panama route over a competing route through Nicaragua.

In 1903, the United States Senate approved the Hay-Herrán Treaty, which agreed to pay the government of Colombia $10 million down and an annual rental of $250,000 for the right to build a six-mile canal zone across its territory, which at the time included Panama. Colombia rejected the proposal and instead demanded $25 million. Irate, Roosevelt in November 1903 secretly supported a successful revolution against Colombian rule, the work of the Panama Canal Company and local rebel groups, which led to the creation of the independent Republic of Panama.[24] To prevent Colombian resistance to the revolution, the United States sent the battleship U.S.S. *Nashville* and other American warships into Panamanian waters. Roosevelt claimed the ships were sent to maintain the free flow of commerce across the isthmus. Three days later, the United States recognized Panama as an independent state, which then approved the Hay-Herrán Treaty, but extended the canal zone to ten miles.

"By far the most important action I took in foreign affairs during the time I was President related to the Panama Canal," Roosevelt wrote in his autobiography.[25] His methods have continued to raise eyebrows, even though TR insisted "that no one connected with the [United States] Government had any part in preparing, inciting, or encouraging the late revolution on the Isthmus of Panama . . . [or] had any previous knowledge of the revolution."[26] Nonetheless, Roosevelt felt that starting work on the Panama Canal was comparable to such major American undertakings as the Louisiana Purchase and the

Dressed in tropical whites, Roosevelt operates a massive steam shovel on his tour of the Panama Canal construction site in 1906. *Theodore Roosevelt Collection, Harvard College Library*

annexation of Texas. Construction of the canal began in mid-1904. Roosevelt went to Panama in 1906 to inspect the work, making him the first president ever to leave the country while in office. The canal was opened to ships in 1914 and officially opened in 1921.

~

DESPITE HIS imperialistic tendencies, Roosevelt was not quite the war-monger that he was made out to be by his critics. He certainly wasn't one to shy away from a conflict if he thought it was in America's national interests, but he was just as comfortable using diplomacy, backed by American military prowess, to bring about his aims.

In foreign affairs, Roosevelt also helped to resolve a dispute over Morocco. He believed that Germany was trying to start a war between Britain and France, and he used an international conference in Spain in 1906 to settle the issue—and stave off World War I for nearly another decade—by promising American support to Britain and France against any German aggression. Roosevelt also dealt with crises in Venezuela and the Dominican Republic, and settled a nettlesome boundary dispute between Alaska and Canada.

To cite the best-known example of his diplomatic work, Roosevelt took a direct role as peacemaker in ending the Russo-Japanese War, which had erupted in 1904 over territorial disputes surrounding Korea and Manchuria (which is now a part of China). Although initially supportive of Japan when it attacked Russia, he became alarmed at its continued victories against Russia and the potential political destabilization of Eastern Europe and Asia. TR helped broker a peace between the two nations in 1905, which made him the first American ever to win the Nobel Peace Prize.

~

THEODORE WON the presidential election of 1904 by a landslide. "Have swept the country by majorities which astound me," Roosevelt wrote. "I had no idea there would be such a sweep."[27] He stepped convincingly out from behind McKinley's shadow, and knowing this would be his last term, he had the most productive years of his presidency. Legend has it that he said right before his inauguration, "Tomorrow I shall come into my office in my own right. Then watch out for me."[28]

His inaugural address, delivered on April 4, 1905 before a crowd that included guests such as the Apache chief Geronimo, sketched out Roosevelt's agenda. He spoke of caring for the needs of fellow Americans and extending the hand of friendship to all nations who shared America's democratic values. "We have duties to others and duties to ourselves; and we can shirk neither," he said.[29] He went on to warn Americans that unrestrained and unregulated capitalism was not a friend of liberty.

The challenge in his second term was to rein in large corporations without giving labor unions too much power or "paralyzing the energies of the business community," and to encourage workers in their efforts to achieve better working conditions. In December 1905, the president proposed to Congress a pure food and drug law, governmental supervision of insurance companies, and an investigation of child labor by the Department of Commerce and Labor. Tighter food laws were spotlighted by the 1906 publication of Upton Sinclair's book, *The Jungle*, a harrowing account of the Chicago meatpacking houses. Roosevelt was personally critical of Sinclair, however, for he felt the writer had been prone to dangerous exaggeration that undercut his integrity as an objective reporter of abuses. He coined the term "muckracker" to describe Sinclair and others whom he felt were as guilty of lying about working conditions in factories as the factory owners were of committing injustices.[30]

While Roosevelt and the American public were reading *The Jungle* and other magazine articles exposing the abuses of "Big business," both real and imagined, the attention of the nation was riveted on the events transpiring in San Francisco. On April 18, 1906, a massive earthquake rocked the city, killing one thousand and leaving nearly 250,000 homeless. When foreign nations offered assistance, however, Roosevelt politely declined because it was his wish that the American people show to the world that under such an adversity the United States would take care of its own; and, spurred on by the indomitable courage which this people have always exhibited under the stress of distracting calamity, set up their flag and build a new city, even though the earth shook beneath its foundations.[31]

On June 16, 1906, as the nation struggled to rebuild San Francisco, Roosevelt signed the act admitting Oklahoma as the nation's forty-sixth state.

Roosevelt was less effective getting his legislative agenda through Congress in the last two years of his presidency because he had lame duck status and Congress chafed at what it saw as an excessive use of executive power. Undaunted, Roosevelt pressed his campaign for reform through finding "an inherent power" in the Constitution to regulate business. In December 1906, he campaigned for laws barring corporations from making contributions to political parties, reducing the hours of railroad workers, and forbidding child labor. At the end of 1908, when Congress restricted the ability of the Secret Service to root out corruption in government, Roosevelt created by executive order an investigatory agency within the Department of Justice. This agency eventually became the FBI.

CHAPTER FOURTEEN

Beyond the White House

As 1909 BEGAN, a colorful chapter of the American presidency was coming to an end. At age fifty, Theodore Roosevelt was soon to become a private citizen once again.

Writing in his autobiography, published four years after he left the White House, Roosevelt said he was satisfied with his political legacy. Comparing his presidency to those of Washington and Lincoln, he argued that the American people were better off in almost every way than they had been when he took office in 1901. TR was especially proud of his economic legacy. Not only had the economy improved, but the federal government seemed leaner and more efficient despite its expanded role in American life:

> One thing is worth pointing out: During the seven and a half years of my Administration we greatly and usefully extended the sphere of Governmental action, and yet we reduced the burden of the taxpayers; for we reduced the interest-bearing debt by more than $90,000,000. To achieve a marked increase in efficiency and at the same time an increase in economy is not an easy feat; but we performed it.[1]

Roosevelt felt his greatest achievements as president were the settlement of the coal strike, the construction of the Panama Canal, the ending of the Russo-Japanese War, and "the toning up of the Government service generally." Many of the basic reforms he proposed became law under succeeding presidents Taft and Wilson, and even some under nephew Franklin D. Roosevelt's New Deal of the 1930s and 40s.

～

AFTER MCKINLEY'S assassination in 1901, Theodore had served out the remaining three and a half years of his term in office. This raised an interesting question. The custom since the time of George Washington had been that a president would not serve more than two terms. Did Roosevelt's partial term in office count as one of the two?

After the election of 1904, Roosevelt was asked that question. "The wise custom which limits the President to two terms," he said, "regards the substance and not the form. Under no circumstances will I be a candidate for or accept another nomination."[2] With such a definitive statement, Theodore Roosevelt refused to run in 1908, even though it was widely predicted that he would win. Instead, he supported Secretary of War William Howard Taft because he believed Taft would continue his policies substantially unaltered. It would be the next best thing to a third Roosevelt administration. Theodore wrote, "if we can elect him President we achieve all that could be achieved by continuing me in office."[3]

Roosevelt campaigned aggressively for Taft. He also gave his friend some advice on how best to win votes and go on the attack against the indefatigable Democrat William Jennings Bryan. Taft went on to win the presidency by a large margin in November 1908, although there was some erosion from Roosevelt's vote totals of four years earlier.

～

ON FEBRUARY 22, 1909, just days before Roosevelt was to leave office, he traveled to Hampton Roads, Virginia, where he welcomed home the sixty ships of the American White Fleet which had just circumnavigated the globe. Roosevelt had assembled the fleet on December 1, 1907. Made up entirely of ships built since the end of the Spanish-American

Roosevelt drags Taft along in the election of 1908, in a cartoon called "The Presidential Handicap." Unable to run himself, Roosevelt was hurt and angry when Taft departed from his policies.

War, the fleet was a show of American naval force to those world powers who, in the words of one biographer, "thought of this country as a land peopled by dollar-chasers, too absorbed in getting rich to think of providing defense for themselves."[4] The fleet was very much a "big stick" that Roosevelt hoped would let the United States continue to "speak softly" in world affairs.

Three days before he left office, Roosevelt held a farewell luncheon for thirty-one out-of-town friends and members of his "Tennis Cabinet." Some wept openly. On March 3, his last full day as president, Roosevelt spent time with congressmen and journalists who came to wish him well. Writer and historian Henry Adams, the grandson and great-grandson of presidents and a well-known critic of various facets of modern life, had trembled with fear when Roosevelt took office in 1901, but he visited him at the White House twice during March, including on his final day in office. "I shall miss you very much," a depressed Adams said, and the two men shook hands.[5] Clearly, Roosevelt had won Adams's admiration.

Inauguration Day—March 4, 1909—came complete with terrible late winter weather. As TR and President-elect Taft arrived at the Capitol, they had to walk through the worst inaugural weather anyone could ever recall. Roosevelt, who was always able to find the humor in a situation, quipped, "I knew there would be a blizzard when I went out."[6]

~

EVEN AS HE HAD begun his second term, there was much speculation about what TR would do once he left office. Some suggested that he run for the Senate in 1908; others suggested that he run for mayor of New York City. What Theodore did was to pick up his pen. He agreed to write twelve articles a year for the *Outlook*, a weekly journal, for the sum of $12,000. He also picked up his rifle. A month after Taft's inauguration, Roosevelt went on a big game hunt with his twenty-year-old son, Kermit, in Mombase, British East Africa (now the Republic of Kenya). Ever the naturalist, he offered his wildlife specimens to the Smithsonian Institution. Andrew Carnegie, the former steel magnate turned philanthropist, paid a large part of the $75,000 for the expedition. Roosevelt, though, paid his own expenses with money from a $50,000 contract he signed with *Scribner's* magazine to write a series of articles about the trip. The articles were later collected into a book, *African Game Trails*.

One reason Roosevelt said he went hunting out of the country was to avoid the impression that he was secretly pulling the strings in the new Taft administration, as some would surely have insinuated. But there was a deeper reason, one that harkened back to Roosevelt's youth, namely, that he needed to face adventure and danger once again. For a vigorous man who had spent most of the past decade under searing public scrutiny in Washington, it must have been a relief to escape, if only for a year.

A number of friends and family members believed that a year of tramping through disease-infested and dangerous jungles in Africa would be the end of Theodore, but he proved them wrong. On March 14, 1910, he met his wife and his daughter, Ethel, in Khartoum, and returned home. He and Kermit had shot 512 animals, including lions, rhinos, and elephants, consisting of 296 species in all. A few in Roosevelt's time, and many more in the years since, have questioned the necessity of hunting. But contemporaries were not so concerned about hunting in the abstract: what angered them about Roosevelt was that he seemed to be an indiscriminate hunter with a lust for killing. As one critic, a Congregationalist minister named William J. Long, quipped, "Every time Mr. Roosevelt gets near the heart of a wild thing he invariably puts a bullet through it."[7] Roosevelt replied to these "nature fakers" (as he called them) that he, too, was opposed to sense-less killing. "Game-butchery," he wrote, "is as objectionable as any other form of wanton cruelty or barbarity. But to protest against all hunting of game is a sign of softness of head, not of soundness of heart."[8] To that end, he insisted that the animals killed during his African safari were used either for food or for scientific purposes.

$$\sim$$

ON THE HOME FRONT, the political machine built by Roosevelt was beginning to show signs of wear. William Howard Taft was hardly the gregarious president Roosevelt had been, and he found it increasingly difficult to live up to Roosevelt's legacy, let alone carry it forward. It didn't help matters that he began to remove Roosevelt loyalists, includ-ing conservationist Gifford Pinchot, from their positions. This angered many Republicans in Congress, most notably Roosevelt's longtime friend, Senator Henry Cabot Lodge. Lodge corresponded with Roosevelt in Africa and kept him abreast of developments.

Taft's political problems continued to grow. Soon enough he stum-bled over the issue of tariff reform by supporting a bill that actually raised the average tariff level, even though Taft had declared himself for lower tariffs. As a result of this blunder and the general perception that Taft was once again aligning the Republican Party with the wealthy powerbrokers who had been so despised by Roosevelt, his popularity level dipped.

Many political observers were commenting by the end of 1909 that Roosevelt could have the Republican presidential nomination in 1912 simply for the asking. When reporters asked if he would run, Roosevelt waved off the question. But he was concerned. After his African safari, Roosevelt went on a tour of Europe, where he was treated as a celebrity. Keeping in touch with political events back home, he wrote angrily to Lodge that Taft and Congress had reversed many of his policies. Taft, who was in many respects Roosevelt's protégé, had turned out to be his own man, and Roosevelt was not pleased.

&

WHEN ROOSEVELT returned to the United States in June 1910, he was even more popular than when he was president. Huge crowds met him as he set foot again on American soil. Congress, in March, had awarded him a $10,000 annual pension. He said he was tired of politics and would be taking a break to spend more time with his family.

Talk began almost immediately about forming a third political party, the Progressive Party, in time for the 1912 elections. Rumor had it that Roosevelt would be asked to be the party's candidate for president. The Progressive movement, which had developed in the second half of the nineteenth century, had at its heart the conviction that unrestrained capitalism and individualism were the cause of the nation's social and economic woes. Progressives proposed instead a number of reforms that stressed collective action, including more government oversight of business, higher wages, women's suffrage, and improved quality of education.

TR was less than excited about running as a third party candidate. A lifelong Republican, he felt certain that he would split the Republican vote and hand the presidency back to the Democrats.

Instead Roosevelt hoped that the Republican Party would adopt progressive ideas. He also met with President Taft and tried to resolve the differences between them.

In late summer 1910, Roosevelt went on an extended speaking tour in the western United States, where he repeated his support for a strong federal government. On August 31, in a speech delivered in Osawatomie, Kansas, Theodore called for a "New Nationalism" that "puts the national need before sectional or personal advantage. This New Nationalism," he said, "regards the executive power as the steward of the public welfare." The speech showed further that Roosevelt had accepted the central thrust of the Progressive movement: that government must play a role in restraining the predatory tendencies of business so that there could be "a more substantial equality of opportunity and reward" in the society as a whole.[9] Accordingly, Roosevelt's progressive agenda included income and inheritance taxes, regulation (but not government ownership) of railroads, and making the right to property subservient to the general welfare.

The 1910 midterm elections were a disaster for the Republicans. The Democrats picked up fifty-eight seats to win control of the House of Representatives for the first time in sixteen years, and the Republican control of the Senate was reduced to the slim majority of ten seats. In New Jersey, Democrat Woodrow Wilson was elected governor and began to entertain thoughts of running for president.

In recent American history, there had been precedent for a former president to run for office again. Grover Cleveland had done it, although he had served initially for only one term. But Roosevelt took the Republican losses in 1910 personally and they knocked some wind out of his sails. He hoped the Democrats' sweeping victory at the polls would end any talk of him running for president in 1912. Privately, he figured that if Taft lost in 1912, he would be in a good position to run again for the presidency in 1916.

Events made it impossible for Roosevelt to wait. In October 1911, the final split between Taft and Roosevelt took place when the Taft administration sued U.S. Steel for being a monopoly. What especially irritated Roosevelt was Taft's claim that Roosevelt had helped the company to become a monopoly. Roosevelt believed his record as president showed that he had broken up unlawful monopolies, and he took Taft's accusations as a personal insult. He barked that Taft "is utterly unfit for leadership, and this is a time when we need leadership."[10]

Roosevelt was finding it harder and harder to say no to running for president against Taft. In February 1912, after seven Republican governors asked him to run, he agreed.

By the summer Theodore had lost the Republican nomination badly, hurt by his own pledge not to seek a second term. He had alienated many old friends. Nonetheless he immediately expressed an interest in running on the ticket of the Progressive Party, which he had founded in 1912 to gather support for his progressive reforms. It was often called the "Bull Moose" party because TR, when asked by a reporter how he was, declared, "I'm feeling like a bull moose." Roosevelt ran against Taft, the Republican nominee, and Woodrow Wilson, the Democratic candidate. His Progressive Party agenda included direct election of senators, votes for women, reduced tariffs, unemployment insurance, old age pensions, abolition of child labor, and pure food laws. During the campaign, Roosevelt argued the case for government activism:

> There was once a time in history when the limitation of governmental power meant increasing liberty for the people. In the present day the limitation of governmental power, of government action, means the enslavement of the people by the great corporations who can only be held in check through the extension of governmental power.[11]

It became clear that the race would be between Roosevelt and Wilson, whom Theodore frequently referred to as "the schoolmaster" because he had served as president of Princeton University. Roosevelt and Wilson shared many progressive views, and Roosevelt had once admitted that Wilson was "an excellent man"[12]—an attitude that changed once Wilson secured the Democratic nomination. Moreover, Wilson's policies began to seem overly radical to Roosevelt, for Wilson favored trust-busting over regulation, and attacked Roosevelt for supporting some monopolies.

As the fall began, TR's campaign train rumbled through the midwestern United States, a Progressive stronghold. On October 14, three weeks before the election, it stopped in Milwaukee. As Roosevelt left his hotel to deliver a rousing campaign speech, he was approached by a man named John Schrank and shot in the chest from six feet away. Schrank believed that Roosevelt's election would turn the United States into a dictatorship.

Doctors examined Roosevelt at the scene and noticed that trajectory of the bullet had been altered by passing through the thick manuscript of the speech in his pocket, as well as by nicking his metal eyeglass case. Rather than hitting his heart, the bullet fractured his fourth rib.

Roosevelt wrote his son, Kermit, a few days later and emphasized that the would-be assassin had failed to do any lasting damage. The bullet was found in the president's chest wall, and because it posed no danger it was allowed to remain. Theodore wrote matter-of-factly, "As I did not cough blood, I was pretty sure the wound was not a fatal one."[13] Remarkably, though, he insisted on delivering his speech, and then spoke for eighty minutes, mostly extemporaneously. The speech became one of the most powerful of his political career. Pierced with agonizing pain, Theodore ascended the podium and began, "I am going to ask you to be very quiet and please excuse me from making a long speech. I'll do the best I can, but there is a bullet in my body."[14] To reinforce his point, he showed the amazed crowd his bloody shirt. As always, Roosevelt had managed to convert his manliness into political capital.

He then continued with his remarks: "I have altogether too important things to think of to feel any concern about my own death . . . I can tell you with absolute truthfulness that I am very much uninterested in whether I am shot or not."[15] After he had said all that was on his mind— which was well after his advisers urged him to stop—Roosevelt went to the hospital. He was released two weeks before the election, which he lost to Woodrow Wilson by over two million votes. President Taft came in third, over a half-million votes behind Roosevelt.

The contest in 1912 between Roosevelt and Wilson was really a contest between two competing schools of thought within the Progressive movement. Roosevelt's "New Nationalism," as outlined in his 1910 speech in Kansas, reiterated many of the themes of his presidency, including more direct government intervention in business. Wilson's "New Freedom," as he called it, was less extreme. He criticized Roosevelt for advocating programs that would foster paternalism in government, which would in turn weaken democratic structures. In the end, voters were more willing to adopt Wilson's agenda.

Roosevelt was gracious in defeat, even philosophical. "I accept the result with entire good humor. As for the Progressive cause, I can only repeat [that] the cause in itself must triumph, for this triumph is essential to the well-being of the American people."[16] He also had advice for his dejected supporters: "The fight is over. We are beaten. There is only one thing to do and that is to go back to the Republican party. You can't hold a party like the Progressive party together. There are no loaves and fishes."[17]

～

THE ELECTION OF 1912 would be Roosevelt's last. He was fifty-five years old. He had made numerous enemies within the party, and many Republicans believed that he had cost Taft the election by siphoning off some traditionally Republican voters. Roosevelt watched, powerless, as President Wilson adopted many of the reform proposals of the Progressive Party and got them through Congress.

His political career over, Roosevelt turned to writing his autobiography, which was published in 1913. That fall, Theodore and Edith took a tour of South America, where he gave a series of lectures at Rio de Janeiro and Buenos Aires and collected animal and botanical specimens. Against the advice of experts, he also chose to venture into the

Incoming president Woodrow Wilson and outgoing president Taft enjoy the
inauguration in March 1913. Roosevelt and his "Bull Moose" party had lost the
1912 election, but TR would go on to criticize Wilson openly for his neutrality in
World War I. *Library of Congress*

perilous and unexplored regions of the Amazon River basin on foot and
by canoe. Dangerous waterfalls surrounded Roosevelt and claimed the
lives of two native guides, and the Roosevelt entourage was harassed by
tropical insects and threatened by piranha inhabiting local freshwater
streams. During the trip, Roosevelt badly injured his leg and developed
malaria. When he returned to New York, the press commented that he
looked frail—he had lost fifty-seven pounds—but that his eyes hadn't
lost any of their fire.

In 1914, as Theodore entered his twilight years alongside his wife and
children, he was as uncertain about his future as ever. But there was little

time for introspection: World War I erupted in Europe with the assassination of Archduke Franz Ferdinand of Austria. Publicly, Roosevelt supported President Wilson's view that the United States should remain neutral in the war. Privately he supported the Allied war effort in Europe and pushed for American preparedness. By early 1915, he was openly urging the United States to enter the war on the side of England, France, and Italy. This brought him into open conflict with the president, and soon he was criticizing Wilson's policy of neutrality as weak and cowardly.

$\sim$

AS ROOSEVELT AGITATED for war, sizable cracks were developing in American relations with Germany. By 1915 no ship, American or not, was immune from harassment or attack by German submarines in the waters of the Atlantic. Even as Roosevelt and many American leaders were pushing for greater American involvement in the war, events took a turn for the worse. On March 28, the British ship *Falaba* was sunk by German U-boats, killing 104, including one American. On May 1, the first American ship to be targeted by the Germans was a tanker called the *Gullfight*; three people were killed, although the ship didn't sink. As Roosevelt wrote to his son, Ted, the North Atlantic would not be retaken by appeasement.

On May 7, 1915, after the German ambassador to the United States warned the ship not to set sail, a German submarine sank the British oceanliner *Lusitania* in the Atlantic Ocean. The ship was carrying 4,200 cases of rifle cartridges for the British army, and witnesses said the resulting massive explosions sunk it in only eighteen minutes. The death toll was high—1,198 killed—but more important for Roosevelt was the fact that 128 American civilians were among the dead. When the news of the *Lusitania*'s sinking broke, Roosevelt thundered, "[Wilson] and [Secretary of State William Jennings] Bryan are morally responsible for the loss of the lives of those American women and children. . . . They are both of them abject creatures and they won't go to war unless they are kicked into it."[18]

Emotions were running high, and initially most Americans whole-heartedly supported Roosevelt's call for action against Germany. The day after the *Lusitania* was sunk, the headline WHAT A PITY ROO-SEVELT IS NOT PRESIDENT was splashed across the front page of the *New York Herald*. In Times Square in New York City, Theodore's old stomping grounds, a large crowd demanded that the United States make a formal declaration of war against Germany. Influential men—including three attorneys general of the United States and Theodore's affluent investment banker son, Ted—wrote President Wilson to demand that the United States enter the war.

Political realities began to sink in for Wilson. He was on the wrong side of public opinion, and he would be seeking reelection the next year. Clearly, he would need to make a gesture of solidarity, even if he stopped short of declaring war. He was helped, as Roosevelt himself acknowledged, by time; the public's war cry, which had been so deafening in the days immediately following the sinking of the *Lusitania*, became something of a whisper. Wilson split the difference and agreed only to increase American military preparedness.

Roosevelt was incensed. In August, he traveled to an old army camp at Plattsburg, New York, to review dozens of men and boys from the higher reaches of society who had paid to train for a month in preparation for war against the Kaiser. The men included the mayor and police commissioner of New York City, the bishop of Rhode Island, and three of Roosevelt's own children—Ted, Archie, and Quentin. The Roosevelt boys, very much their father's children, had subscribed to his view of manliness; they could not run from a fight, especially if it came to them. Roosevelt spoke for an hour to encourage the men, and later he wrote that the camp was a "glimmer of hope" for America.

Across the country, young men who were eager to help the Allies—and impatient with America's reluctance about entering the war—joined the British or Canadian forces in order to see action. One was Roosevelt's second son, Kermit, who wrote to his father, "I don't like the war at all because of Belle and Kim [his wife and infant son], but as long as it's going on I want to be the first in it."[19]

Soon news came that the Germans had sunk the British oceanliner *Arabic* off the coast of Ireland, killing two Americans. President Wilson's closest military advisers—including his secretary of state, secretary of war, and a certain assistant secretary of the navy named Franklin D. Roosevelt—were beginning to believe that TR was right. American diplomacy was not resolving the war in Europe, and Wilson was becoming isolated within his own administration.

Privately, Roosevelt wondered if he should have waited until 1916 to make another run for the presidency. But he knew that he had spent his remaining political capital running as a Progressive Party candidate in 1912, which split the Republican vote and put Wilson in the White House. This time, he did not want to be a third party spoiler. The Republican candidate in 1916 was Justice Charles Evans Hughes, who had resigned from the Supreme Court to run for president. Roosevelt declined the Progressive Party's nomination and urged his supporters to back Hughes.

It was to no avail. Hughes, as Taft before him, was not the dynamic candidate Roosevelt had been, and Americans showed that they were not angry enough at Germany to remove President Wilson from office. The chief Democratic campaign slogan—"He kept us out of war"—resonated with enough voters to give Wilson a slim majority of 600,000 votes. So close was the election, however, that Hughes went to bed on election night convinced that he had won. The truth became known early the next morning, when it was announced Wilson had won California and thus had secured a majority in the electoral college.

~

ON DECEMBER 18, 1916, President Wilson urged that the world must work for "peace without victory" if it hoped to end the war. Roosevelt continued to insist that the Germans would only stop fighting on terms favorable to them. Shortly after Wilson's speech, the Germans offered something they hoped would prevent the Americans from entering the war. Although they reasserted their right to sink any foreign ship in the Atlantic, they allowed the Americans to send one ship a week to Falmouth, England outside the danger of being attacked. The ship was to take a carefully prescribed course, had to fly a particular flag, and must be painted the color mandated by the Germans.

This direct challenge to American dignity could not be allowed to stand. And when it became known that Germany was seeking military alliances with Mexico and Japan, Wilson had no other options available to him. Bowing to intense public pressure, Wilson buckled, and he broke off relations with Germany on April 6, 1917. In his war speech to Congress, Wilson charged, "The world must be made safe for democracy."

Despite his hatred of what he considered Wilson's halfhearted attitude, Theodore believed in showing the Germans a united and determined American front. Therefore once President Wilson had declared war, Roosevelt pulled back his criticism of the administration and closed ranks behind Wilson. In a meeting with Wilson, Roosevelt offered to bury the hatchet. "Mr. President," he said, "what I have said and thought, and what others have said and thought, is dust in a windy street, if we can now make your [war] message good."[20]

Roosevelt did all he could to unite the country behind the war. Itching to get back into combat, he wrote to the War Department and offered to lead a volunteer force to Europe, as he had done to Cuba twenty years earlier, but he was turned down. When Roosevelt's offer became known, as many as 300,000 men offered to serve in combat under the man known the world over as the Colonel, even though he was now fifty-nine years old.

Congress instituted the draft on May 18, prompting Roosevelt to try once more. He appealed directly to President Wilson and asked to lead four divisions of troops overseas. Wilson denied his request, saying that volunteer troops had no place on the modern battlefield. Roosevelt wasn't convinced: "President Wilson's reasons for refusing my offer had nothing to do either with military considerations or with public needs."[21][*]

His friend and biographer, William Roscoe Thayer, later wrote, "I believe that no greater disappointment ever came to him than when he was prohibited from going out to battle in 1917."[22] The French, whose land was being drenched with the blood of war, were desperate that Roosevelt, a visible sign of American intervention, be allowed to serve. French premier Georges Clemenceau, for one, demanded, "Send Roosevelt!" But Roosevelt's push to lead troops into battle was not for nothing:

> Roosevelt . . . was gratified to learn from good authority that his efforts in the spring of 1917 to secure a commission and lead troops over seas were the immediate cause of the sending of any American troops. President Wilson, it was reported, had no intention, when we went to war, of risking American lives over there . . . But Roosevelt's insistence and the great mass of volunteers who begged to be allowed to join his divisions, if they were organized, awakened the President to the fact that the American people expected our country to give valid military support to the Allies, at death-grapple with the [Germans].[23]

All four of Roosevelt's sons fought in Europe. Ted became a lieutenant colonel, Kermit and Archibald became captains, and Quentin became a lieutenant. Quentin, who zealously memorized the eye chart in order to pass his military physical, was killed in a dogfight with seven German planes over France on July 14, 1918. The ebullient youngest son, the one who looked most like his father—in addition to poor eyesight, he was stocky and round-faced—was gone forever. Friends and family members remarked later that Roosevelt never recovered from the loss of his youngest son. In the days following his death, Roosevelt wore a black armband. In tribute to Quentin, TR wrote:

---

[*] Although Roosevelt was not allowed to fight at an advanced age, his son, Ted, was the oldest man to land on the beach at Normandy, France, during the 1944 Allied D-Day invasion. He was fifty-seven years old.

TR's popularity resonated with Americans well after his presidency, and he continued to use it to promote the rightness of his causes. Taken in 1912, this picture conveys how Roosevelt went directly to the people, and was loved in return. *Theodore Roosevelt Collection, Harvard College Library.*

> Both life and death are parts of the same Great Adventure . . . The torches whose flame is brightest are borne by the gallant men at the front . . . These men are high of soul, as they face their fate on the shell-shattered earth, or in the skies above or in the waters beneath . . . These are the torch-bearers; these are they who have dared the Great Adventure.[24]

Not able to fight himself, Theodore toured the country on behalf of the war effort. He called for Americans to support the Red Cross and to buy government Liberty bonds. Roosevelt himself bought $60,000 worth of bonds, and he sent 200 pairs of shoes to Archie's company stationed in Europe. Theodore also wrote a syndicated weekly newspaper column in the *Kansas City Star* supporting an all-out, united effort to win the war. While respecting the rights of nonviolent conscientious objectors, he also advocated both rich and poor being drafted to fight overseas.

Roosevelt's high profile support for American involvement in World War I once again made him the frontrunner for the Republican presidential nomination in 1920. This time TR welcomed the idea. Although the contest was still a few years away, he sounded more and more like a candidate. In his speeches he came out in favor of old age pensions, sickness and unemployment insurance, public housing projects, reduction of working hours, aid to the farmer, and the regulation of large corporations.

"The Colonel" was preparing himself for one last campaign. He told his sister of his intentions: "Corinne, I have only one fight left in me, and I think I should reserve my strength in case I am needed in 1920."[25] After years on the political periphery, Roosevelt hoped that he would once again be able to take center stage.

CHAPTER FIFTEEN

The End Comes

EVEN AS HE THOUGHT about one last run for office, the injuries Theodore had sustained while touring South America a few years earlier had developed complications. Now nearly sixty, Roosevelt was plagued by rheumatic fever, and in February 1918 he was sent to the hospital for an emergency operation on the abscesses that had developed on his leg and thigh. Uncharacteristically, he stayed in the hospital for a month. (The bullet that remained in his chest apparently had caused no lasting damage. A year after he was shot, Roosevelt wrote, "I do not mind it [the bullet] any more than if it were in my waistcoat pocket!"[1])

Theodore had trouble with his balance, had lost hearing in his left ear, and was blind in one eye as a result of the boxing match while president. Still, he remained a force on the political scene. It seemed that Roosevelt's national stature as a cheerleader for the American war effort had been enough to cover a multitude of his past sins against the Republican Party.

Even though he was in the hospital and his health was failing, "the Republican leader of one of the Atlantic states and a former Progressive leader of one of the Pacific states" came to inquire about Roosevelt's interest in running for president in 1920. He was the only man who could defeat Wilson, they argued. Would he run? After giving the matter some thought, Roosevelt said, "Yes, I will run if the people want me, but only if they want me. I will not lift a finger for the nomination." One of the men replied, "Colonel, it will be yours, without strings, and on your own terms."[2]

But Roosevelt really was in no condition to consider another run for the White House. By November, his inflammatory rheumatism was so bad that his feet were swollen and he could no longer wear shoes. Family members began to worry that the end was near.

Roosevelt's last public speech was given at Carnegie Hall in New York City on November 2, 1918. The topic was "The American Negro and the War." He spoke passionately and eloquently about the many black soldiers who served with distinction in the Spanish-American War, as well as in the current conflict. Then, perhaps thinking back to how he was criticized for having Booker T. Washington to dinner at the White House in 1901, he issued a call for an end to racism in American society:

> I don't ask for any man that he shall, because of his race, be given any privilege. All I ask is that in his ordinary civil and political rights, in his right to work, to enjoy life and liberty and the pursuit of happiness, that as regards these rights he be given the treatment that we would give him if he was an equally good man of another color.[3]

Three days later, Roosevelt violated doctor's orders not to get out of bed and he journeyed a mile to the polls to vote. In the 1918 midterm elections, the Republicans won majorities in both houses of Congress. Roosevelt was very much in a triumphant mood. "[Wilson] demanded a vote of confidence. The people voted a want of confidence, by returning to each House of Congress a majority of the Republican Party of which I am one of the leaders."[4]

His assessment of the changed political dynamic in the United States was affirmed six days later, on November 11, when Germany surrendered unconditionally. World War I was over, but Roosevelt was once again in the hospital—for treatment of anemia, vertigo, and fever—when word of the German surrender came. Some suggested that Roosevelt waited until the German surrender before he himself surrendered to the demands of physicians.

For the next seven weeks, Roosevelt wrote letters, maintained his weekly column, and continued his policy disputes with President Wilson. One day, while Corinne was visiting him, he told her that he had made a promise to himself at age twenty-one to "work up to the hilt until I was sixty, and I have done it."[5] He seemed to her to be ready to die, but that didn't stop him from planning a fishing expedition to the Gulf of Mexico for the following March.

Equipped with a wheelchair, Theodore was released from the hospital on Christmas Day, 1918. When his doctor warned that he might be confined to a wheelchair for the rest of his life, Roosevelt replied that it would take more than a wheelchair to stop him from working. Sadly, though, he was too frail to play Santa Claus for the children of a local public school, which he had done each year for several decades.

Back home in Long Island, TR was a shell of his former self. Now he tired easily, his joints were stiff, and he spent afternoons resting on the sofa. On Sunday, January 5, 1919, he edited several newspaper articles and finished a column expressing reservations about Wilson's idea for a League of Nations. According to his wife, as night approached Roosevelt looked out the window and seemed to be at peace.

At ten o'clock Roosevelt told Edith that he felt as if he was dying. Then he tried to reassure her, saying that he was probably wrong. At eleven o'clock that evening he completed his day's work, and his long-time personal assistant, James Amos, helped him to bed. A short time later Theodore asked Amos to put out the light. Earlier that evening, what would become Roosevelt's final words to the American people were read aloud to a crowd at a benefit at the Hippodrome in New York: "I cannot be with you; and so all I can do is wish you Godspeed."[6]

Five hours later, at four o'clock in the morning, Amos noted Roosevelt's irregular breathing and called for his nurse. By the time the nurse arrived, Theodore was dead, the result of an embolism, a blood

Theodore Roosevelt, 1915. In his late fifties, he was contemplating a run for the presidency in 1920, though the years had taken their toll on his health. Photograph by Walter Scott Shinn. *Theodore Roosevelt Collection, Harvard College Library*

clot in his coronary artery. "The old lion is dead," Archie cabled his brothers Ted and Kermit, who were stationed near Coblenz, Germany.[7]

A towering figure in American politics for nearly forty years had finally been silenced. And typically, he died on his own terms, at Sagamore Hill, among the mounted animal heads and shelves of books, where he felt most at home. As news of his death spread, words of praise and appreciation poured into Sagamore Hill. Speaking for many, President Wilson wrote, "In his death the United States has lost one of its most distinguished and patriotic citizens."[8]

∽

A FEW DAYS LATER, on January 8, Roosevelt was laid to rest in a small graveyard overlooking Oyster Bay. His wife, who died in 1948 at age eighty-seven, was buried alongside him. Friends, family, old Rough Riders, and various government officials attended his funeral services in the nearby chapel. "The services," a friend wrote, "were most impressive in their simplicity, in their sense of intimacy, in the sentiment that filled the hour and the place of personal loss and of pride of possession of a priceless memory."[9] Tears flowed freely as those in attendance realized that, in addition to losing a dear friend and colleague, the nation and the world had lost one of its most beloved and complex leaders. Perhaps fittingly, the Roosevelt grave lies next to a bird sanctuary.

After the church services, pallbearers, walking through the dusting of snow on the grounds, took Roosevelt's coffin to his final resting place. "Death had to take him sleeping," said Vice President Marshall in his eulogy, "for if Roosevelt had been awake, there would have been a fight."[10]

Epilogue

As a family, the Roosevelts became part of New York's elite soon upon arriving in America, and they never looked back. In time, they would send three of their own—Theodore Roosevelt and his nephew, Franklin Roosevelt, and his niece Eleanor (Elliott's daughter) as first lady—to the White House. These Roosevelts left an indelible mark on the American consciousness as it was forged through war and in peace.

In 1939, Theodore Roosevelt's contributions to the United States were memorialized when his face was carved in the exposed granite of Mount Rushmore in the Black Hills of South Dakota. Sculptor Gutzon Borglum chose Roosevelt—promoter of the Panama Canal, conservationist, and business reformer—as one of the four presidents who helped most to make the United States into a great nation. Next to Roosevelt on Mount Rushmore are three other great leaders— George Washington, Thomas Jefferson, and Abraham Lincoln. That Roosevelt was chosen to share the memorial with such illustrious men is itself a tribute to his many and varied contributions to American society.

In 1962, Sagamore Hill and Theodore's boyhood home in New York City were established as national historic sites, and they still draw about 100,000 visitors annually. The Theodore Roosevelt National Memorial Park, established in 1947, a year before Edith's death, includes Roosevelt's beloved Elkhorn Ranch in the Badlands of North

Dakota. A navy aircraft carrier, the U.S.S. *Theodore Roosevelt*, also bears his name.

Theodore Roosevelt was larger than life, a towering figure in his time, a true American original. The words of friend and biographer Hermann Hagedorn, written shortly after Roosevelt's death, still hold true today:

> He was not a second Washington. He was not a second Lincoln . . . . He was not a second anybody. He was Theodore Roosevelt himself, unique. There has never been anybody like him in the past, and, though the world wait a long while, there will never be any one like him in the future.[1]

Notes

Books that appear with full citations in the Selected Bibliography appear here with author, title, and page numbers only; otherwise, full citations are given in the first note of each chapter. Thereafter, all citations in each chapter are shortened for ease of reference.

Epigraph

1. *The Moving Picture World* (October 22, 1910), p. 920.

Introduction

1. William Roscoe Thayer, *Theodore Roosevelt*, pp. 262–63.

2. Edwyn Sandys, "Our Sportsman President," *Field and Stream* (Dec. 1901)

3. See Thomas G. West, *Vindicating the Founders: Race, Sex, Class, and Justice in the Origins of America* (Lanham, Md.: Rowman & Littlefield, 1997), pp. 1–36.

4. Abraham Lincoln, Speech at Alton, 15 October 1858, in *The Lincoln-Douglas Debates of 1858*, ed. Robert W. Johannsen (New York: Oxford University Press, 1965), p. 311, quoted in West, *Vindicating*, p. 32.

5. Andrew Carnegie, *Triumphant Democracy* (1885), quoted in Paul Johnson, *A History of the American People* (New York: HarperCollins, 1997), p. 555.

Chapter One: New Birth

1. Wm. Draper Lewis, *The Life of Theodore Roosevelt* (n.p.: The United Publishers, 1919), p. 25.

2. Hermann Hagedorn, *The Roosevelt Family of Sagamore Hill*, p. 183.

3. *Harper's Weekly*, 11 April 1857, quoted in John A. Kouwenhoven, ed. *Adventures of America—1857–1900: A Pictorial Record from Harper's Weekly* (New York: Harper & Brothers, 1938), p. 1.

4. Quoted in Winthrop D. Jordan et al., *The United States*, 6th combined ed. (Englewood Cliffs, N.J.: Prentice-Hall, 1987), p. 477.

5. *Harper's Weekly* (1860), quoted in Kouwenhoven, *Adventures*, p. 23.

6. Quoted in Edmund Morris, *The Rise of Theodore Roosevelt*, p. 32.

7. Theodore Roosevelt, *Autobiography*, p. 17.

8. Quoted in Lewis, *Life*, p. 35.

9. Hermann Hagedorn, *The Boys' Life of Theodore Roosevelt*, pp. 13–14.

10. Ibid., p. 15.

Chapter Two: Mind and Body

1. Corinne Robinson, *My Brother Theodore Roosevelt* (New York: Scribner's, 1921), p. 50, quoted in Edmund Morris, *The Rise of Theodore Roosevelt*, p. 60.

2. Ibid.

3. Hermann Hagedorn, *The Roosevelt Family of Sagamore Hill*, p. 5.

4. Louise Vierick, *Success Magazine* (October 1905), quoted in Morris, *Rise*, p. 73.

5. Theodore Roosevelt, Private Diary, 16 November 1869, quoted in Morris, *Rise*, p. 122.

6. Theodore Roosevelt to S. West, 15 February 1868, quoted in H.W. Brands, *T.R.: The Last Romantic*, p. 51.

7. Theodore Roosevelt, *Autobiography*, p. 23.

8. Memorandum by Arthur H. Cutler, quoted in Morris, *Rise*, p. 75.

9. Ibid.

10. Roosevelt, *Autobiography*, pp. 23–24.

11. Theodore Roosevelt, *Letters*, 1:13, quoted in Carleton Putnam, *Theodore Roosevelt, Vol. 1: The Formative Years, 1858–1886*, p. 127.

Chapter Three: Phoenix Rising

1. William Roscoe Thayer, *Theodore Roosevelt*, p. 15.

2. Donald Wilhelm, *Theodore Roosevelt as an Undergraduate* (Boston, 1910), p. 35, quoted in Paul F. Boller, Jr., *Presidential Anecdotes* (New York: Penguin, 1982), p. 201.

3. Boller, *Anecdotes*, p. 22.

4. Theodore Roosevelt, Private Diary, 15 March 1877, quoted in H.W. Brands, *T.R.: The Last Romantic*, p. 85.

5. Theodore Roosevelt, Private Diary, 9 June 1878, quoted in Edmund Morris, *The Rise of Theodore Roosevelt*, p. 95.

6. Theodore Roosevelt, Private Diary, 1 September 1878, quoted in Carleton Putnam, *Theodore Roosevelt, Vol. 1: The Formative Years, 1858–1886*, p. 150.

7. Theodore Roosevelt, Private Diary, date not given, quoted in Putnam, *Theodore Roosevelt*, p. 151.

8. Theodore Roosevelt to Anna Roosevelt Cowles, 20 September 1886, quoted in Betty Boyd Caroli, *The Roosevelt Women* (New York: Basic Books, 1998), p. 81.

Chapter Four: "My Own Sweet, Pretty Darling"

1. Theodore Roosevelt to John Roosevelt, 25 February 1880, quoted in Edmund Morris, *The Rise of Theodore Roosevelt*, p. 104.

2. Quoted in Henry F. Pringle, *Theodore Roosevelt*, p. 30.

3. Ibid.

4. Theodore Roosevelt, Private Diary, 25 January 1880, quoted in Morris, *Rise*, p. 123.

5. Alice Lee to Martha Bulloch Roosevelt, 3 February 1880, quoted in Morris, *Rise*, p. 124.

6. Theodore Roosevelt, *Autobiography*, p. 24.

7. Theodore Roosevelt, Private Diary, 5 May 1880, quoted in H.W. Brands, *T.R.: The Last Romantic*, p. 104.

8. William Roscoe Thayer, *Theodore Roosevelt*, p. 18.

9. Hermann Hagedorn, *The Boys' Life of Theodore Roosevelt*, p. 63.

10. Quoted in Ferdinand C. Iglehart, *Theodore Roosevelt: The Man as I Knew Him*, p. 85.

11. Theodore Roosevelt, Private Diary, 18 August 1879, quoted in Morris, *Rise*, p. 117.

12. Theodore Roosevelt, *Letters*, 1:43, quoted in Carleton Putnam, *Theodore Roosevelt, Vol. 1: The Formative Years, 1858–1886*, p. 178.

13. Theodore Roosevelt, Private Diary, 25 March 1880, quoted in Morris, *Rise*, p. 127.

14. Thayer, *Theodore Roosevelt*, p. 21.

15. Fanny Smith, Private Diary, 27 October 1880, quoted in Morris, *Rise*, p. 136.

16. Putnam, *Theodore Roosevelt*, p. 210.

17. Ibid., pp. 210–211.

18. Theodore Roosevelt, Private Diary, 4 November 1880, quoted in Brands, *T.R.*, p. 110.

Chapter Five: Law, Then Politics

1. Theodore Roosevelt, Private Diary, 18 March 1881, quoted in Edmund Morris, *The Rise of Theodore Roosevelt*, p. 137.

2. Theodore Roosevelt, *Autobiography*, p. 55.

3. Walter Rauschenbusch, *Christianity and the Social Crisis* (New York: Macmillan, 1907), p. 422, quoted in Sydney E. Ahlstrom, *A Religious History of the American People*, Vol. 2 (Garden City, N.Y.: Image, 1975), p. 250.

4. Quoted in Carleton Putnam, *Theodore Roosevelt, Vol. 1: The Formative Years, 1858–1886*, p. 219.

5. Theodore Roosevelt, Private Diary, 11 December 1880, quoted in Morris, *Rise*, p. 141.

6. Quoted in Morris, *Rise*, p. 244.

7. Robert G. Caldwell, *James A. Garfield: Party Chieftan* (New York, 1931), p. 298, quoted in Paul F. Boller, Jr., *Presidential Campaigns* (New York: Oxford University Press, 1985), p. 142.

8. Roosevelt, *Autobiography*, p. 57.

9. Ibid., pp. 60–61.

10. Theodore Roosevelt, Private Diary, 5–6 July 1881, quoted in H.W. Brands, *T.R.: The Last Romantic*, p. 125.

11. Quoted in Morris, *Rise*, p. 152.

12. William Roscoe Thayer, *Theodore Roosevelt*, pp. 32–33.

Chapter Six: On to Albany

1. Theodore Roosevelt, *Autobiography*, p. 89.

2. Quoted in Carleton Putnam, *Theodore Roosevelt, Vol. 1: The Formative Years, 1858–1886*, p. 250.

3. Theodore Roosevelt, Private Diary, 3 January 1882, quoted in Edmund Morris, *The Rise of Theodore Roosevelt*, p. 163.

4. Theodore Roosevelt, Private Diary, 7 January 1882, quoted in H.W. Brands, *T.R.: The Last Romantic*, p. 131.

5. Roosevelt, *Autobiography*, p. 90.

6. Theodore Roosevelt, Private Diary, 14 February 1882, quoted in Morris, *Rise*, p. 169.

7. Roosevelt, *Autobiography*, p. 91.

8. Quoted in Ferdinand C. Iglehart, *Theodore Roosevelt: The Man As I Knew Him*, p. 101.

9. Quoted in Putnam, *Theodore Roosevelt*, p. 275.

10. Roosevelt, *Works*, 14:12–14, quoted in Putnam, *Theodore Roosevelt*, p. 277.

11. Roosevelt, *Letters*, 1:58, quoted in Putnam, *Theodore Roosevelt*, p. 278 n. 15.

12. Roosevelt, *Works*, 14:25, quoted in Putnam, *Theodore Roosevelt*, p. 300.

13. Roosevelt, *Autobiography*, p. 81.

14. Ibid., p. 83.

15. *New York World*, 3 March 1883, quoted in Putnam, *Theodore Roosevelt*, p. 285.

Chapter Seven: "The Light Has Gone Out of My Life"

1. Theodore Roosevelt to Alice Lee Roosevelt, 20 September 1883, quoted in H.W. Brands, *T.R.: The Last Romantic*, p. 158.

2. Theodore Roosevelt, *A Book-Lover's Holidays in the Open* (New York: Charles Scribner's Sons, 1916) <http://www.bartelby.com/57/> (25 November 2001)

3. Theodore Roosevelt, *Autobiography*, p. 94.

4. Quoted in Edmund Morris, *The Rise of Theodore Roosevelt*, p. 240.

5. Ibid., p. 241.

6. Theodore Roosevelt, Private Diary, 14 February 1884, quoted in Morris, *Rise*, p. 241.

7. Morris, *Rise*, p. 243.

8. Quoted in Michael Teague, *Mrs. L: Conversations with Alice Roosevelt Longworth*, pp. 10, 12.

9. Ibid., p. 5.

10. Privately published memorial to Alice Lee Roosevelt, quoted in Morris, *Rise*, p. 391.

11. Roosevelt, *Autobiography*, p. 88.

12. Quoted in Carleton Putnam, *Theodore Roosevelt, Vol. 1: The Formative Years, 1858–1886*, pp. 490–91.

13. Roosevelt, *Autobiography*, p. 88.

14. Worthington Chauncey Ford, ed., *Letters of Henry Adams* (Boston and New York: Houghton Mifflin, 1930), p. 360, quoted in Winthrop D. Jordan et al., *The United States*, 6th combined ed. (Englewood Cliffs, N.J.: Prentice-Hall, 1987), p. 459.

Chapter Eight. A Breath of Fresh Air

1. William Roscoe Thayer, *Theodore Roosevelt*, pp. 59–60.

2. Roosevelt, *Works*, 1:386, quoted in Edmund Morris, *The Rise of Theodore Roosevelt*, p. 326.

3. Thayer, *Theodore Roosevelt*, p. 62.

4. See M.L. Avery, *Dixie After the War* (New York, 1906), p. 286, and Richard W. Gilder, *Grover Cleveland: A Record of Friendship* (New York, 1910), p. 218, cited by Paul F. Boller, Jr., *Presidential Campaigns* (New York: Oxford University Press, 1985), p. 156.

5. Sylvia Morris, *Edith Kermit Roosevelt* (New York: Coward, McCann, 1980), p. 77, quoted in Carol Felsenthal, *Princess Alice: The Life and Times of Alice Roosevelt Longworth*, p. 33.

6. Quoted in Hermann Hagedorn, *The Roosevelt Family of Sagamore Hill*, p. 18.

7. Ibid.

8. Morris, *Edith Kermit Roosevelt*, pp. 89–90, quoted in Felsenthal, *Princess Alice*, p. 35.

9. Theodore Roosevelt to Anna Roosevelt, 20 September 1886, quoted in Felsenthal, *Princess Alice*, p. 35.

10. Lilian Rixey, *Bamie* (New York: McKay, 1963), p. 68, quoted in Felsenthal, *Princess Alice*, pp. 36–37.

11. Quoted in David McCullough, *Mornings on Horseback*, p. 359.

12. Quoted in Michael Teague, *Mrs. L: Conversations with Alice Roosevelt Longworth*, p. 12.

13. Quoted in Hagedorn, *Roosevelt Family*, p. 50.

14. Bill Sewall, *Bill Sewall's Story of T.R.* (New York and London: Harper & Brothers, 1919), p. 93.

15. Paul Johnson, *A History of the American People* (New York: HarperCollins, 1997), p. 616.

16. Theodore Roosevelt to Anna Roosevelt, 22 August 1888, quoted in H.W. Brands, *T.R.: The Last Romantic*, p. 217.

17. Quoted in Felsenthal, *Princess Alice*, p. 45.

18. Theodore Roosevelt to Emily Carow, 16 August 1903, quoted in Edward J. Renehan, Jr., *The Lion's Pride: Theodore Roosevelt and His Family in Peace and War*, p. 11.

19. Thayer, *Theodore Roosevelt*, p. 261.

20. Theodore Roosevelt, *Autobiography*, pp. 18–19.

21. Quoted in Hagedorn, *Roosevelt Family*, p. 31.

22. Quoted in Teague, *Mrs. L*, p. 44.

23. Roosevelt, *Autobiography*, p. 349.

24. Theodore Roosevelt, *Harper's Weekly* (March 1893), quoted in Morris, *Rise*, pp. 383–84.

25. The club has an official web site at <http://www.boone-crockett.org/>.

Chapter Nine: Cleaning Up the System

1. Theodore Roosevelt to Brander Matthews, 5 October 1888, quoted in Edmund Morris, *The Rise of Theodore Roosevelt*, p. 389.

2. Quoted in Henry F. Pringle, *Theodore Roosevelt*, p. 86.

3. Roosevelt, *Letters*, 1:167, quoted in Morris, *Rise*, p. 404.

4. Roosevelt, *Letters*, 1:168, quoted in Morris, *Rise*, p. 405.

5. Theodore Roosevelt to Anna Roosevelt, 17 December 1893, quoted in H.W. Brands, *T.R.: The Last Romantic*, p. 256.

6. Theodore Roosevelt, *Autobiography*, p. 172.

7. Ibid., p. 175.

8. Lincoln Steffens, *Autobiography* (New York: Harcourt Brace, 1936), p. 257, quoted in Morris, *Rise*, p. 482.

9. Roosevelt, *Letters*, 1:458, quoted in Morris, *Rise*, p. 491.

10. Roosevelt, *Autobiography*, p. 177.

11. Hermann Hagedorn, *The Boys' Life of Theodore Roosevelt*, p. 167.

12. Jacob Riis, *How the Other Half Lives* (1890; reprint, New York: Hill and Wang, 1957), p. 1.

13. Ibid., pp. 2–3.

14. Roosevelt, *Autobiography*, p. 64.

15. Ibid., pp. 204–05.

16. Henry Cabot Lodge to Theodore Roosevelt, 31 August 1895, quoted in Morris, *Rise*, p. 508.

17. Steffens, *Autobiography*, p. 258, quoted in Morris, *Rise*, p. 510.

Chapter Ten: America at War

1. Quoted in Mark Sullivan, *Our Times*, p. 169.

2. Theodore Roosevelt to Henry Cabot Lodge, 26 February 1896, quoted in Edmund Morris, *The Rise of Theodore Roosevelt*, p. 537.

3. Quoted in Henry F. Pringle, *Theodore Roosevelt*, p. 114.

4. Quoted in Ferdinand C. Iglehart, *Theodore Roosevelt: The Man as I Knew Him*, p. 121.

5. Quoted in Edward J. Renehan, Jr., "Speech Delivered by Edward J. Renehan, Jr., at the 80th Annual Dinner of the Theodore Roosevelt Association."

6. Frederick Jackson Turner, *The Significance of the Frontier in American History* (1893), quoted in John W. Kirshon, ed., *Chronicle of America* (Mount Kisco, N.Y.: Chronicle Publications, n.d.), p. 501.

7. Quoted in Judith Freeman Clark, *America's Gilded Age: An Eyewitness History* (New York: Facts on File, 1992), p. 162.

8. Theodore Roosevelt, "Annual Message to Congress" (6 December 1904), in *A Compilation of the Messages and Papers of the Presidents* (New York: Bureau of National Literature, 1906), vol. 16, pp. 7053–7054, quoted in Thomas A. Bailey and David M. Kennedy, eds., *The American Spirit*, 8th ed., vol. 2 (Lexington, Mass.: D.C. Heath and Company, 1994), pp. 176–77.

9. Theodore Roosevelt to Benjamin J. Diblee, 16 February 1898, quoted in Morris, *Rise*, p. 600.

10. Henry W. Elson, *Side Lights on American History*, vol. II (1900; reprint, Washington, D.C.: Regnery, 1999), p. 350.

11. Archie Butt, *The Letters of Archie Butt, Personal Aide to President Roosevelt* (New York: Doubleday, 1924), p. 146, quoted in H.W. Brands, *T.R.: The Last Romantic*, p. 335.

12. Theodore Roosevelt, *The Rough Riders*, p. 94.

13. Theodore Roosevelt to Corinne Roosevelt, 25 June 1898, quoted in Brands, *T.R.*, p. 349.

14. Quoted in Dale L. Walker, *The Boys of '98: Theodore Roosevelt and the Rough Riders*, p. 281.

15. Mark Twain, "Anti-Imperialist Homecoming," in Jim Zwick, ed., *Mark Twain: Weapons of Satire: Anti-Imperialist Writings in the United States, 1898–1935* <http://www.boondocksnet.com/ail98–35.html> (10 November 2001).

16. Quoted in Michael Teague, *Mrs. L: Conversations with Alice Roosevelt Longworth*, p. 48.

Chapter Eleven: Governor and Vice President

1. For a detailed account of the controversy, see Mitchell Yockelson, "'I Am Entitled to the Medal of Honor and I Want It': Theodore Roosevelt and His Quest for Glory," *Prologue: Quarterly of the National Archives and Records Administration* (Spring 1998), vol. 30, no. 1 <http://www.nara.gov/publications/prologue/trmedal1.html> (9 March 2002).

2. Henry F. Pringle, *Theodore Roosevelt*, rev. ed., p. 142.

3. Ibid., p. 144.

4. Quoted in Hermann Hagedorn, *The Roosevelt Family of Sagamore Hill*, p. 75.

5. *Public Papers of Theodore Roosevelt, Governor* (Albany, 1899–1900), pp. 248–49, quoted in Edmund Morris, *The Rise of Theodore Roosevelt*, p. 691.

6. Quoted in Pringle, *Theodore Roosevelt*, p. 149.

7. William Roscoe Thayer, *Theodore Roosevelt*, p. 202.

8. Quoted in Ferdinand C. Iglehart, *Theodore Roosevelt: The Man as I Knew Him*, p. 127.

9. Quoted in Theodore Roosevelt, *The Rough Riders*, p. 37.

10. William Allen White, *Autobiography* (New York: Macmillan, 1946), p. 327.

11. Elting E. Morison and John Blum, eds., *The Letters of Theodore Roosevelt*, 8 vols. (Cambridge, Mass.: Harvard University Press, 1951–54), p. 1023, quoted in Morris, *Rise*, p. 705.

12. Theodore Roosevelt to Thomas C. Platt, 1 February 1900, quoted in H.W. Brands, *T.R.: The Last Romantic*, p. 393.

13. Quoted in Pringle, *Theodore Roosevelt*, p. 156.

14. Quoted in Evan Cornog, *Hat's in the Ring: An Illustrated History of American Presidential Campaigns* (New York: Random House, 2000), p. 165.

15. Theodore Roosevelt, "Vice Presidential Inaugural Address," March 1901 <http://www.usahistory.com/presidents/th-ro2.htm> (25 November 2001).

16. Ibid.

17. Theodore Roosevelt to Leonard Wood, 17 April 1901, quoted in Brands, *T.R.*, pp. 410–11.

18. Theodore Roosevelt, *Autobiography*, p. 364.

19. Quoted in Roger Butterfield, *The American Past: A History of the United States from Concord to the Great Society*, p. 317.

20. Ibid., p. 313.

Chapter Twelve: Life in the White House

1. Quoted in William Roscoe Thayer, *Theodore Roosevelt*, p. 273.

2. William Marion Reedy in *St. Louis Mirror*, 19 December 1901, quoted in Edmund Morris, *Theodore Rex*, p. 80.

3. Quoted in Maurice Francis Egan, "Theodore Roosevelt in Retrospect," *The Atlantic Monthly* (May 1919) <http://www.theatlantic.com/issues/19may/egan.html> (8 March 2002).

4. Quoted in Thayer, *Theodore Roosevelt*, p. 260.

5. Ibid., p. 269.

6. Ibid., p. 276.

7. Ibid., pp. 265–66.

8. Quoted in Editors of Time-Life Books, *This Fabulous Century – Volume I: 1900–1910* (New York: Time-Life Books, 1969), p. 61.

9. Owen Wister, *Roosevelt: The Story of a Friendship* (New York, 1930), p. 87, quoted in Paul F. Boller, Jr., *Presidential Anecdotes* (New York: Penguin, 1982), p. 206.

10. Quoted in Time-Life Books, *This Fabulous Century*, p. 66.

11. Quoted in Michael Teague, *Mrs. L: Conversations with Alice Roosevelt Longworth*, p. 70.

12. Ibid., p. 66.

13. Ibid., p. 129.

14. Quoted in Hermann Hagedorn, *The Roosevelt Family of Sagamore Hill*, pp. 195–96.

15. Theodore Roosevelt, *Autobiography*, p. 356.

16. Thayer, *Theodore Roosevelt*, pp. 267–68.

17. Quoted in Roger Butterfield, *The American Past: A History of the United States from Concord to the Great Society*, rev. ed., p. 316.

18. Quoted in Ferdinand C. Iglehart, *Theodore Roosevelt: The Man as I Knew Him*, p. 168.

19. Quoted in Teague, *Mrs. L*, p. 44.

20. Hagedorn, *Roosevelt Family*, p. 144.

21. Ibid., p. 134.

22. Ibid., p. 136.

Chapter Thirteen: President Roosevelt

1. William Roscoe Thayer, *Theodore Roosevelt*, p. 283.

2. Quoted in Henry F. Pringle, *Theodore Roosevelt*, rev. ed., p. 175.

3. Quoted in Mark Sullivan, *Our Times*, p. 261.

4. Ibid., pp. 258–59.

5. Quoted in Ernest R. May et al., *The Life History of the United States*,

Volume 9: 1901–1907 – The Progressive Era (New York: Time Inc., 1964), p. 13.

6. Thayer, *Theodore Roosevelt*, p. 203.

7. Lewis L. Gould, *The Presidency of Theodore Roosevelt* (Lawrence: University of Kansas Press, 1991), p. 28, cited in Edmund Morris, *Theodore Rex*, p. 29.

8. William Elsey Connelley, *A Standard History of Kansas and Kansans* (Chicago: Lewis Publishing Co., 1918), vol. 2, p. 1167, quoted in Linda R. Monk, ed., *Ordinary Americans* (Alexandria, Va.: Close Up Publishing, 1994), pp. 128–29.

9. Quoted in Ferdinand C. Iglehart, *Theodore Roosevelt: The Man as I Knew Him*, p. 198.

10. Quoted in George E. Mowry, *The Era of Theodore Roosevelt and the Birth of Modern America*, p. 131.

11. Cited in Arthur S. Link, *American Epoch: A History of the United States Since the 1890s* (New York: Knopf, 1955), p. 48.

12. Theodore Roosevelt, *Autobiography*, pp. 445–46.

13. Quoted in Roger Butterfield, *The American Past: A History of the United States from Concord to the Great Society*, p. 320.

14. Theodore Roosevelt, "Message to the Fifty-seventh Congress," quoted in E.E. Garrison, comp., *The Roosevelt Doctrine* (New York: Robert Grier Cooke, 1904), p. 33.

15. Theodore Roosevelt to Carrol D. Wright, 13 August 1904, quoted in Mowry, *Era*, p. 141.

16. Roosevelt, *Autobiography*, pp. 485–86.

17. Quoted in Michael Teague, *Mrs. L: Conversations with Alice Roosevelt Longworth* (New York: Doubleday, 1981), p. 113.

18. Quoted in Theodore Roosevelt Association, "Theodore Roosevelt: Conservationist" <http://www.theodoreroosevelt.org/conservation.html> (14 November 2001).

19. Roosevelt, *Autobiography*, p. 410.

20. Theodore Roosevelt, "Message to the Fifty-seventh Congress," quoted in E.E. Garrison, *The Roosevelt Doctrine*, pp. 148–49.

21. Thayer, *Theodore Roosevelt*, p. 237.

22. Quoted in John Milton Cooper, Jr., *Pivotal Decades: The United States, 1900–1920*, p. 106.

23. Thayer, *Theodore Roosevelt*, pp. 178–79.

24. Theodore Roosevelt to Dr. Albert Shaw, quoted in Thomas A. Bailey and David M. Kennedy, eds., *The American Spirit*, 8th ed., vol. 2 (Lexington, Mass.: D.C. Heath and Company, 1994), pp. 191–92.

25. Roosevelt, *Autobiography*, p. 526.

26. Theodore Roosevelt, "Special Message to Congress," 4 January 1904, quoted in Garrison, *The Roosevelt Doctrine*, p. 73.

27. Theodore Roosevelt to Henry Cabot Lodge, 9–10 November 1904, quoted in H.W. Brands, *T.R.: The Last Romantic*, p. 513.

28. Quoted in Mowry, *Era*, p. 197.

29. Theodore Roosevelt, "Second Inaugural Address," 4 March 1905 <http://www.bartleby.com/124/pres42.html> (14 November 2001).

30. Theodore Roosevelt "The Man with the Muck-Rake," *Putnam's Monthly and the Critic* 1 (October 1906), pp. 42–43, in Bailey and Kennedy, *The American Spirit*, pp. 202–03.

31. Quoted in Walter Lord, *The Good Years: From 1900 to the First World War*, p. 148.

Chapter Fourteen: Beyond the White House

1. Theodore Roosevelt, *Autobiography*, p. 384.

2. *Washington Post*, 9 November 1904, quoted in H.W. Brands, *T.R.: The Last Romantic*, p. 514.

3. Theodore Roosevelt to George Trevelyan, 19 June 1908, quoted in Brands, *T.R.*, p. 629.

4. William Roscoe Thayer, *Theodore Roosevelt*, p. 288.

5. Quoted in Henry F. Pringle, *Theodore Roosevelt*, rev. ed., p. 348.

6. *New York Times*, 5 March 1909, quoted in Edmund Morris, *Theodore Rex*, p. 551.

7. Mark Sullivan, *Our Times: The United States 1900–1925*, 3:155, quoted in Brands, *T.R.*, p. 651.

8. Theodore Roosevelt, *African Game Trails*, pp. 13–14, quoted in Brands, *T.R.*, p. 651.

9. Quoted in Pringle, *Theodore Roosevelt*, p. 381.

10. Theodore Roosevelt to C. Willard, 11 December 1911, quoted in Brands, *T.R.*, p. 698.

11. Quoted in *Progressive Principles: Selections from Addresses Made During the Presidential Campaign of 1912*, ed. Elmer H. Youngman (New York: Progressive National Service, 1913), p. 217, quoted in Bailey and Kennedy, *The American Spirit*, p. 226.

12. Theodore Roosevelt to C. Osborn, 5 July 1912, quoted in Brands, *T.R.*, p. 718.

13. Theodore Roosevelt to Kermit Roosevelt, 19 October 1912, quoted in Brands, *T.R.*, p. 721.

14. Quoted in Pringle, *Theodore Roosevelt*, p. 399.

15. Quoted in Brands, *T.R.*, p. 271.

16. Quoted in Pringle, *Theodore Roosevelt*, p. 400.

17. Ibid.

18. Theodore Roosevelt to Archibald Roosevelt, 19 May 1915, quoted in Brands, *T.R.*, p. 756.

19. Quoted in Edward J. Renehan, Jr., *The Lion's Pride: Theodore Roosevelt and His Family in Peace and War*, p. 133.

20. Theodore Roosevelt to J. O'Laughlin, 13 April 1917, quoted in Brands, *T.R.*, p. 781.

21. Quoted in Thayer, *Theodore Roosevelt*, p. 433.

22. Ibid., p. 434.

23. Ibid., p. 442.

24. Quoted in Pringle, *Theodore Roosevelt*, p. 421.

25. Corinne Roosevelt Robinson, *My Brother Theodore Roosevelt* (New York: Scribner's, 1921), pp. 346–47, quoted in Brands, *T.R.*, p. 810.

Chapter Fifteen: The End Comes

1. Quoted in Webb Garrison, *A Treasury of White House Tales* (Nashville: Rutledge Hill Press, 1996), p. 36.

2. Quoted in Hermann Hagedorn, *The Boys' Life of Theodore Roosevelt*, pp. 381–82.

3. Theodore Roosevelt, "The American Negro and the War," 2 November 1918, quoted in Edward J. Renehan, Jr., *The Lion's Pride: Theodore Roosevelt and His Family in Peace and War*, p. 216.

4. Theodore Roosevelt to Arthur Balfour, 10 December 1918, quoted in H.W. Brands, *T.R: The Last Romantic*, p. 809.

5. Corinne Roosevelt Robinson, *My Brother Theodore Roosevelt* (New York: Scribner's, 1921), pp. 362–63, quoted in Brands, *T.R.*, pp. 810–11.

6. Quoted in "Theodore Roosevelt," *Time* (3 March 1958) <http://www.time.com/time100/leaders/profile/troosevelt_related.html> (8 March 2002).

7. Quoted in Brands, *T.R.*, p. 811.

8. Quoted in Ferdinand C. Iglehart, *Theodore Roosevelt: The Man as I Knew Him*, p. 350.

9. William Roscoe Thayer, *Theodore Roosevelt*, p. 450.

10. bid.

Epilogue

1. Hermann Hagedorn, *The Boys' Life of Theodore Roosevelt*, pp. 1–2.

Selected Bibliography

Auchincloss, Louis. *Theodore Roosevelt*. New York: Holt/Times, 2001.

Brands, H. W. *T.R.: The Last Romantic*. New York: BasicBooks, 1997.

Butterfield, Roger. *The American Past: A History of the United States from Concord to the Great Society*. Rev. Ed. New York: Simon and Schuster, 1966.

Cooper, John Milton, Jr. *Pivotal Decades. The United States, 1900–1920*. New York: W.W. Norton, 1990.

Crichton, Judy. *America 1900: The Turning Point*. New York: Henry Holt, 1998.

Felsenthal, Carol. *Princess Alice: The Life and Times of Alice Roosevelt Longworth*. New York: St. Martin's, 1988.

Gardner, Joseph L. *Departing Glory: Theodore Roosevelt as Ex-President*. New York: Charles Scribner's Sons, 1973.

Hagedorn, Hermann. *The Boys' Life of Theodore Roosevelt*. New York and London: Harper & Brothers, 1922.

_____. *The Roosevelt Family of Sagamore Hill*. New York: Macmillan, 1954.

Iglehart, Ferdinand C. *Theodore Roosevelt: The Man as I Knew Him*. New York: Christian Herald, 1919.

Lorant, Stefan. *The Life and Times of Theodore Roosevelt*. Garden City, N.Y.: Doubleday & Company, 1959.

Lord, Walter. *The Good Years: From 1900 to the First World War*. New York: Harper & Brothers, 1960.

Manners, William. *TR and Will: A Friendship That Split the Republican Party*. New York: Harcourt, Brace & World, 1969.

McCullough, David. *Mornings on Horseback*. New York: Simon and Schuster, 1981.

Miller, Nathan. *The Roosevelt Chronicles*. Garden City, N.Y.: Doubleday, 1979.

_____. *Theodore Roosevelt: A Life*. New York: William Morrow and Company, 1992.

Morris, Edmund. *The Rise of Theodore Roosevelt*. New York: Coward, McCann & Geoghegan, 1979.

_____. *Theodore Rex*. New York: Random House, 2001.

Mowry, George E. *The Era of Theodore Roosevelt and the Birth of Modern America: 1900–1912*. New York: Harper Torchbooks, 1962.

_____. *Theodore Roosevelt and the Progressive Movement*. Madison: University of Wisconsin Press, 1946.

Pringle, Henry F. *Theodore Roosevelt*. Rev. Ed. San Diego: Harcourt Brace & Company, 1956.

Putnam, Carleton. *Theodore Roosevelt. Volume 1: The Formative Years, 1858–1886*. New York: Charles Scribner's Sons, 1958.

Renehan, Edward J. *The Lion's Pride: Theodore Roosevelt and His Family in Peace and War*. New York: Oxford University Press, 1998.

_____. "Speech Delivered by Edward J. Renehan, Jr., at the 80th Annual Dinner of the Theodore Roosevelt Association," 29 October 1998, Norfolk, Virginia <http://www.theodoreroosevelt.org/life/TRandNavy.htm> (10 November 2001).

Riis, Jacob. *How the Other Half Lives*. 1890. Reprint, New York: Hill and Wang, 1957. Available online at: <http://www.bartleby.com/208/>.

Roosevelt, Theodore. *Autobiography*. 1913. Reprint, New York: Da Capo, 1985. Available online at: <http://www.bartleby.com/55/>.
_____, with additional text by Richard Bak. *The Rough Riders*. 1898. Reprint, Dallas: Taylor Publishing, 1997. Available online at: <http://www.bartleby.com/51/\>.

Sandys, Edwyn. "Our Sportsman President," *Field and Stream*, Dec. 1901<http://www.fieldandstream.com/looking_back/19971104.html> (21 November 2001).

Stanwood, Edward. *A History of the Presidency: 1897–1916*. Boston: Houghton Mifflin, 1928. Reprint, Clifton, N.J.: Augustus M. Kelley, 1975.

Sullivan, Mark, edited and with additional text by Dan Rather. *Our Times*. New York: Scribner, 1996.

Teague, Michael. *Mrs. L: Conversations with Alice Roosevelt Longworth*. New York: Doubleday, 1981.

Teichmann, Howard. *Alice: The Life and Times of Alice Roosevelt Longworth*. Englewood Cliffs, N.J.: Prentice-Hall, 1979.

Thayer, William Roscoe. *Theodore Roosevelt*. Boston: Houghton Mifflin, 1919. Available online at <http://www.bartleby.com/170/>.

Walker, Dale L. *The Boys of '98: Theodore Roosevelt and the Rough Riders*. New York: Tom Doherty Associates, 1998.

FOR MORE INFORMATION

Fritz, Jean. *Bully for You, Teddy Roosevelt!* (New York: G. P. Putnam's Sons, 1991). This brief biography is a solid introduction to the highlights of Roosevelt's life.

Garraty, John A. *Theodore Roosevelt: The Strenuous Life*. (New York: American Heritage Publishing Company, 1967). This nicely illustrated volume strikes a good balance between the simplistic and overly detailed.

Hagedorn, Hermann. *The Boys' Life of Theodore Roosevelt*. (New York: Harper and Brothers, 1918, 1922). This classic book was written by a friend of Roosevelt, and it remains one of the best introductions to Theodore's life and times.

Lord, Walter. *The Good Years: From 1900 to the First World War* (New York: Harper & Brothers, 1960). Lord's book remains one of the best and most readable one-volume accounts of this period. The book is loaded with primary source material, some of which is unavailable elsewhere.

Riis, Jacob. *Theodore Roosevelt, the Citizen*. (New York: The Outlook Company, 1904, available online at: http://www.bartleby.com/206/). This biography by one of Roosevelt's closest friends reveals the personal side of a very public man.

Sullivan, Mark. *Our Times* (New York: Scribner's, 1926–1935). This classic six-volume work provides rich detail on the first few decades of twentieth-century American life, including Roosevelt's presidency.

Theodore Roosevelt Association. "Home Page." <http://www.theodoreroosevelt.org>. This is the official web site of the Theodore Roosevelt Association. It offers a rich collection of photos and essays that illuminate the life and legacy of Theodore Roosevelt.

Welsbacher, Anne. *Theodore Roosevelt*. (Minneapolis: Abdo & Daughters, 1998). This is another brief biography that ably covers the main points of Roosevelt's life.

Zwick, Jim, ed. "Anti-Imperialism in the United States, 1880–1935." <http://www.boondocksnet.com/ail98–35.html>. This web site offers an impressive array of documents that present another perspective on the military exploits of the United States in the late nineteenth and early twentieth centuries.

INDEX

For ease of reference, the entry
for Theodore Roosevelt is divided
into three parts: Political Life,
Private Life, and Works of.